Puppets: Ministry Magic

By Dale and Liz VonSeggen

Group *Books*

Loveland, Colorado

Dedication

We dedicate this book to the many adult leaders and teen puppeteers who have been a part of the puppet ministry at Denver First Church of the Nazarene since 1978.

The V.I.P. Puppet Team (Victory In Puppetry) has taught us what successful puppet ministry is all about through their faithfulness to weekly rehearsals, willingness to work hard and loyalty to God and the team.

May we all be as puppets in God's hands!

Puppets: Ministry Magic
Copyright © 1990 by Dale and Liz VonSeggen

Credits
Edited by Michael D. Warden
Cover and book designed by Judy Bienick

Scripture quotations are from the Holy Bible, New International Version. Copyright © 1973, 1978, 1984 International Bible Society. Used by permission of Zondervan Bible Publishers.

Library of Congress Cataloging-in-Publication Data
VonSeggen, Dale.
      Puppets : ministry magic / by Dale and Liz VonSeggen.
         p. cm.
      ISBN 0-931529-65-4
      1. Puppets and puppet-plays in Christian education.
  I. VonSeggen, Liz. II. Title.
  BV1535.V65 1990
  246'.7—dc20   90-30964
                                                    CIP
                                                    AC

16 15 14 13 12   04 03 02 01 00

Printed in the United States of America.

Visit our Web site: www.grouppublishing.com

Contents

Introduction

Puppets have caught the attention of audiences down through history, helping people laugh, pretend, dream, empathize and learn new ideas. In the past 20 years, puppets have invaded the church. Teenage groups, families, teachers, missionaries and others around the world are discovering an effective "work of their hands" through puppet ministry.

But just what is puppet ministry? It can be different things to different people. It can be a segment of a youth group, where several kids and a director use puppets to reach out to children, the handicapped, those in nursing homes or other youth groups.

Some youth groups use puppets in inner-city ministries and on mission trips to Indian reservations. Others sponsor neighborhood "backyard Bible clubs" in the summer to reach children who may otherwise never hear of Jesus.

Youth choirs and singing groups often use puppets to add variety, drama and excitement to choir tours and performances.

Several puppet teams have each remodeled a church bus and installed carpeting, a sound system and a puppet stage in the back end of the bus. Then they've used the brightly painted, attention-getting vehicle as a mobile puppet theater. They drive the "puppet bus" into parks and neighborhoods to entertain and inspire children and adults.

Countless churches, groups and individuals have discovered that a handful of foam rubber, fake fur and cloth can become a ministry tool with eternal results. And puppet ministry provides opportunities for young people to share their faith and to learn how to work together.

One youth minister writes: "Puppet ministry brings kids into an effective method of outreach and teaches teens to think beyond themselves. As teens realize the impact their work has on the listeners, it causes them to take the message they present more seriously themselves."

One pastor noted the effect puppet ministry had on two painfully shy teenagers in his church: "Through the puppet ministry and the love and care of the director, I watched these two individuals blossom, becoming more and more the people that God made them to be."

Kids who've been actively involved in puppet ministry have expressed their delight in the joy an audience experiences. One teenager said it this way: "The laughter of an audience, the smile on a child's face, the excitement of performing, the outstanding purpose—doing it for God ... All these things make puppetry so special and worthwhile."

So what about you and your church? Why not join the many who've discovered puppet ministry for themselves. All it takes is a puppet or two and a heart for ministry.

How to Use This Book

This book takes you step by step through establishing a puppet ministry in your church or youth group. The guidelines and tips in these pages will help you:

- develop a vision for puppet ministry in your church;
- recruit kids and adults to commit to puppet ministry;
- involve kids in directing the ministry;
- choose your puppets;
- choose scripts;
- write scripts;
- build a puppet stage;
- plan effective rehearsals; and
- put together a complete program.

We'll even give you instructions for taking your puppet team on the road—touching lives by presenting programs to a variety of audiences.

Whether you have teenagers beating down your door for a chance to work with puppets or you're starting out solo, this book provides the tools you need to take puppetry into your church and community. Take an afternoon or two and thoroughly read the entire book. Treat it as a workbook. Highlight critical points. Scribble notes and comments in the margins. Bend it. Stuff it in your pocket or purse. It's okay. It's here to serve you.

But whatever you do, don't leave it lying on the shelf! Let the book act as your guide through the many decisions you must make.

Puppetry has been a lasting source of joy and challenge for us in the many years we've worked in it. The lighthearted message of love conveyed by puppets rarely fails in getting people to open up and look at their hearts. And often it leads them to the one who can meet their every need: Jesus.

That's what makes puppets and puppetry fun and meaningful. So enjoy! Catch the puppet ministry vision and share it with those around you. Before long you'll find yourself sharing God's love through your hands.

CHAPTER 1

Why Puppet Ministry?

When Keith Loy suggested starting a puppet team, his youth group's first reaction was negative—kids thought puppetry was "a dumb idea." But Keith convinced a women's organization in the church to buy five professional puppets for the youth group. After a hands-on test, seven junior highers agreed to begin rehearsals for their new puppet team.

Kids' excitement grew as Keith provided high-quality props and a top-notch stage. Church members and other teenagers began to encourage the team more enthusiastically after it performed a few songs and skits for the congregation.

The small group of puppeteers recruited other junior highers to join them. Soon the whole junior high group was involved in some way—working with sound, stage construction or puppets. Keith set up Bible studies to teach kids about sharing the gospel, and team members began creating their own puppet skits for children, peers and adults. The following summer the puppet team toured Nebraska and South Dakota, doing 10 puppet performances.

According to the teenagers, puppetry changed their youth group from a gathering of individuals to a unified team.

Benefits of Puppet Ministry

When someone views a puppet presentation, he or she sees only the end result of hours spent building stages and props and rehearsing. Since puppetry is lighthearted and fun, people often fail to realize not only the work that goes into it but also the long-lasting—even eternal—results it can have in people's lives.

An active puppet ministry can provide a means to disciple teenagers who're interested in performing and developing a ministry in the church and community. Unlike drama or choir, puppetry allows shy, non-verbal or non-musical teenagers to excel in a performance field and find an effective way to minister. Of course, outgoing teenagers will also enjoy the unique fun of puppetry and the ministry it can have.

A well-rounded, effective puppet ministry focuses on three areas: the group, the church and the community.

Ministry in the group—Since puppet ministry is generally a small group effort, make the puppet team and its rehearsals a place where team members can share prayer requests and personal concerns, and learn to care for others.

Many teams spend 15 to 30 minutes at the beginning of every rehearsal for Bible study or sharing time. Other groups establish prayer partners within the team. Often team members go on fun events together—just as friends. Without this openness and personal concern for each other within the team, outside ministries will be less effective.

As team members rehearse, build props, travel together, pray, and share experiences in a small group setting, many positive things happen. Kids gain self-confidence, learn to reach out to new people and grow in their understanding of themselves and God.

Ministry in the church—Often, puppet ministry in the local church is put into a box labeled "For Children Only," and many exciting avenues for ministry close off. Puppets work well as tools to minister, teach and entertain all ages. You only need to choose skits and songs appropriate to the audience you want to reach. Use puppet ministry in your children's church, Sunday school classes, adult banquets and parties, youth group meetings, worship services, after-church gatherings and senior adult activities.

Ministry to the community—The puppet team is a "natural" when it comes to making an impact outside the walls of the church.

Active puppet ministries often find open doors to minister in places other ministry forms find difficult. For example, puppets are usually welcomed into public schools and many civic clubs or organizations—places evangelists or even Christian drama groups might find hard to penetrate. The fantasy aspect of puppetry makes it seem less "threatening" than other forms of Christian outreach. And the results—in terms of puppeteers' lives and the lives of those they touch—are immeasurable.

A Philosophy of Puppet Ministry

Puppets are wonderful fantasy characters who can take audiences on enchanting trips into the imagination. Fun is their foundation and exaggeration is their primary tool. But behind all the curtains and props, successful puppetry relies on several basic principles. Let's look at these.

Puppets are fantasy characters. They don't have a heart or a soul. They can be compared to cartoon characters such as Bugs Bunny or Mickey Mouse. They aren't real.

For this reason, puppets never "get saved." However, a puppet may sometimes take on the role of a character who's a Christian or even act out a scene in which a character becomes a Christian. But the puppet itself should never ask Jesus into its heart—it doesn't have one!

Here's an example to help clarify this issue. Let's say you have a puppet you generally call Roscoe. Now since Roscoe is a puppet, he should never pray for salvation or go through any kind of conversion experience. However, in a particular skit, Roscoe may play the part of the Apostle Paul on the road to Damascus. In that case, Roscoe would act out Paul's conversion—but only as a puppet imitating a real person.

Puppets don't model negative behavior as acceptable. This includes name-calling, hitting or using bad language. Of course, a puppet may act the part of an evil character who puts down Christianity and challenges the truth. But it should be obvious that the character's attitudes and behavior are wrong.

Puppets don't misuse humor. Puppets usually find success whenever they use humor, but a performance must never make light of spiritual truths. A sprinkling of good humor is usually more effective than a constant barrage of jokes strung through a presentation.

A presentation may start with light material or use a light piece somewhere in the middle for comic relief. But it must end with a serious point. Closing songs and skits should have a thoughtful impact on the audience—not leave them laughing hysterically. Compromising your message for humor diminishes your ministry's effectiveness.

● ● ●

These principles can help you when planning presentations. Good puppetry is good theater. Keep your purpose in mind as you prepare, then work creatively to build God's kingdom in your church and community through puppets.

CHAPTER 2

Getting Started

Kim, a youthworker, saw a puppet team perform once when she visited her sister's church. The performance sparked an idea. Wouldn't a puppet team be great for *her* youth group? So when she returned home, she put together a flier announcing the new puppet team. She talked to her kids about what a great ministry it would be to their church and community. She encouraged everyone to get involved.

About a week later, the new team had its first rehearsal. A few kids came—some out of genuine interest, others just out of curiosity. Kim had borrowed puppets from a neighboring church, and the kids played with them for about an hour.

The team met for four more weeks, then disbanded.

What went wrong? Although the puppets were fun, the team had no sense of direction or purpose. And they were disappointed that more kids didn't come. Kim didn't answer several important questions before she jumped into puppet ministry. For instance, how big should the team be? How will I recruit my members? Who's going to be on the team? What will the team do once it's together? You need to answer questions like these before you take your kids into a rehearsal.

The Team Size

Your puppet team may have any number of members, but a team with five to eight kids and one or two adult directors usually works best. If your church has several adults to help lead, you might choose to have 12 to 15 members. But keep the team small at first so you can work more effectively with each puppeteer. Then increase numbers as performance skills and commitment increase.

How do you get potential puppeteers through the door? You can spark interest in several ways. For example, invite a quality puppet team to perform. Take your teenagers to see a puppet team rehearse. Or better yet, attend a puppet ministry training seminar.

Evaluate your church's situation to determine how you'll recruit your team. Some leaders hold auditions. But one-on-one recruiting often works best. Some leaders also talk to all their kids and parents together, then build their team with those who'll commit to an ongoing puppet team ministry.

The Team Members

How should a puppet team be put together? Who should be involved? It all depends on the situation. Puppet teams come in all shapes and sizes—some with just two kids the same age, others with 30 kids ranging from ages 12 to 18. However, certain membership combinations work better than others.

For example, puppet teams usually work best when members are about the same age. This makes it easier to select the size of puppets and height of the stage so everyone can participate. Also, it's harder to build team spirit with a broader age span. A team with members from seventh grade through high school will work, but two teams would work better—one for junior high and one for high school.

Anyone can become an excellent puppeteer. But certain kids are particularly drawn to this ministry.

Do you have any shy kids in your youth group? They're perfect puppetry prospects. Since all the performing happens behind a curtain, puppetry gives quiet kids a great creative outlet. Puppetry also builds their self-confidence.

Other potential puppeteers are kids who like music but really don't like to—or can't—sing. Puppetry may be just the place for these kids to get involved. They can perform without singing.

The youth group's drama buffs or "hams" are other good prospects. Puppetry is a natural outlet for these kids.

Perhaps your group includes a "loner." Since puppet teams are small, tightknit groups, they can become exactly what a lonely teenager needs to form friendships.

Probably the most important advice for the beginning puppet director is: "Get help!" Recruit assistance for the many jobs involved in puppet ministry. Adults or kids with sound equipment experience, artistic ability, sewing expertise, organizational skills and even counseling ability will be invaluable to the ministry.

Many kids have hidden talents a puppet ministry could utilize. Also, giving kids responsibility gives them more "ownership" in the ministry.

Kids can fill many roles in your puppet team:
- putting together and running the sound system;
- putting together and running the lighting system;
- booking performances;
- making props;
- making puppets and puppet costumes;
- designing scenery;
- writing scripts;
- acting as "puppet caretakers";
- driving puppeteers to a performance;
- working with publicity;
- sponsoring a party or refreshments after rehearsal; or
- leading devotions or sharing personal testimonies.

As the team director, recruit enough leaders so if you were removed from the picture, the ministry would continue. Too often a puppet team's leadership focuses on one individual. And if that individual moves away, loses interest or becomes discouraged, the ministry dies.

When recruiting adult leaders, look first to the puppeteers' parents. They're often your best prospects. Beyond them, ask young couples, singles, senior adults or those who've been involved in puppetry or drama in the past.

The Defined Ministry

When Don began a puppet ministry team three years ago, many group members were skeptical. They weren't convinced that using puppets was an effective way to minister. But the puppet team has grown into a powerful ministry.

Among other accomplishments, Don's team has:

● taken two summer ministry tours;
● performed several full-length musicals;
● performed in area public schools; and
● hosted a training festival for kids from area churches.

But Don's team hasn't done everything. For example, Don's team has never:

● performed in a nursing home;
● performed in a prison or a juvenile home;
● worked with kids in children's hospitals; or
● worked with clients in a mental institution.

Why? Because Don and his team defined their ministry before they ever started. They didn't try to do too much and were able to work effectively with the groups they concentrated on.

The primary motivations for any puppet ministry are to encourage Christians in their faith and to share Christ with others. But other reasons can also encourage you to start a puppet ministry in your church, such as:

● involving kids in a relational, hands-on ministry;
● reaching out to the community;
● training kids to share their faith; or
● enhancing existing church programs.

Although any puppet team can do all these things to some degree, no team can do everything—all the time. That's why you and your team need to develop a mission statement for your ministry. Pray extensively with your team. Have team members decide exactly what the puppet ministry will look like and what it'll do. Discuss your mission with your puppeteers and church leaders. Guide your team in determining *why* the ministry exists, then compose a mission statement that'll help you accomplish that "why." See the "Sample Mission Statement" on page 16.

Post your team's mission statement prominently in your

church, so you'll all be constantly reminded of your purpose and have less chance of being sidetracked by less important things.

Sample Mission Statement

The Praise-Hands puppet team is an ongoing ministry of First Church that strives to encourage Christians in their faith and to share the gospel with non-Christians. Praise-Hands works primarily with area churches and social organizations.

Your Role as Director

Once your team has defined your puppet ministry mission statement, you're ready to dig in to the week-to-week workings of a puppet ministry team—almost. Before you race off in a mad frenzy to purchase puppets and set up a rehearsal schedule, let's look at your role as the director of this exciting new ministry.

The puppet ministry's success depends largely on the director's enthusiasm, commitment and organization. It's your job to motivate the team members and helpers, and to keep the ministry on track. And just how do you do that? Consider these simple tips.

Maintain a positive attitude. Enthusiasm is contagious! One of the best ways to keep your group excited is to keep yourself excited. Pray daily, thanking God for what he has done in your puppet ministry. And tell the kids often why you're thankful for the puppet team.

Encourage your team members. Kids get worn down every day—at school, with their friends, even at home. So make puppet rehearsal an encouraging time for kids. Don't overly criticize kids' performance at rehearsal. A simple rule to follow is to say 10 positive things about a puppeteer's performance for every criticism.

Build relationships. Puppetry isn't the only thing in your team members' lives. Take time to get to know the kids, learn about their interests and talk with them about their problems. Be available to help them with homework. Invite individual team members out for a soft drink occasionally.

Strive for excellence. Kids don't want to be embarrassed about what they do. So push kids to do their best. They'll take more pride in what they're doing.

Pace your workload. Discouragement often comes when there's too much to do and not enough time to do it. Keep track of kids' schedules, and avoid having them memorize long scripts while they're busy with exams at school or with extracurricular activities. Allow plenty of rehearsal time before each performance.

Have fun. Puppetry is sometimes hard work, but it never has to be boring. Design fun into your rehearsals. Include games, refreshments and free time. Even have parties after the rehearsals.

A Question of Money

Many ingredients of puppet ministry—puppets, stage, sound equipment, tapes and scripts—require money. So to keep your new puppet ministry afloat, you need a financial plan.

You can usually adjust a puppet ministry's cost to fit your budget. For example, you can purchase materials for a stage, or you can improvise with temporary or simplified stages. Likewise, you can purchase printed scripts, recorded scripts or songs designed specifically for puppets to perform. Or you can write your own scripts and record them yourselves.

Don't feel you must purchase every item immediately. Begin small and build slowly as the Holy Spirit and your money allow.

Check these options to raise funds for your new puppet ministry.

Fund-raisers—Many puppet groups do fund-raisers and establish a "puppet fund" to pay for supplies. Carwashes, bake sales, even "puppet-thons" (kids puppeteering for long

Your Puppet Team's Name

Okay, so you've got your puppet ministry started. Now, what're you going to call it? Just giving a puppet ministry a name helps define it.

Choose a name that's sharp enough so kids aren't "turned off" by it, yet stay true to the focus of your ministry. Peruse this list of puppet team names from across the country. Perhaps these will spark your creativity:

Christ's Cloth Company	Heaven's Hand-E-Work
F Troop (Faith)	Zacchaeus & Company
V.I.P. (Victory In Puppetry)	Sunnyside Bunch
Free Spirit Puppets	The Joy Company
M & M (Miniature Ministers)	The Puppet Parade
Salt and Light Company	The Rainbow Bunch
Power and Light Company	The King's Farm Family
Sonshine Gang	New Life Puppets
New Creation Puppets	Happy Hands
God's Handful	Midget Missionaries
Everlasting Arms	Heaven's Handful

By the way, avoid the word "Muppet" in your puppet team's name, or when describing the puppets you use. Muppet is a copyrighted trademark name belonging to Jim Henson Productions. Henson coined the term in 1955 to describe creations such as Kermit and Miss Piggy.

Once you choose your team's name, create T-shirts, sweat shirts or team jackets with your team's name and logo on it. This creates team spirit and builds excitement.

hours) are effective fund-raisers.

Church budget item—Some church budgets allocate money each year for puppet ministry. If you draw up a long-term ministry plan and present it to your church board, you may find that your church would be pleased to support an ongoing puppet ministry.

Gifts and donations—Often individuals or families will gladly support a puppet ministry financially. Get permission from your church to send a letter to all the members explaining what puppet ministry is about and how they can help.

Puppet adoption—Many churches use an "Adopt a Puppet" program to raise money. First, make or purchase one puppet. Then use this puppet in a church service to make an announcement challenging families, individuals, Sunday school classes or other groups to donate enough money to make or purchase other puppets.

When the first benefactor agrees to donate the required money, publish his or her name in the church bulletin. When the new puppet arrives, take a picture of the new puppet and its sponsor. Then give the sponsor a "Certificate of Adoption."

This approach can also encourage other groups in the church to sponsor puppets. Suggest that church groups follow themes in the adoption process. For example, the senior adult group could adopt a "grandpa" and "grandma" puppet, or a missions group could sponsor multicultural puppets.

Paid performances—After a puppet team has mastered basic puppetry techniques and developed a repertoire, take opportunities to perform outside the church. In many of these situations, your group may receive love offerings or honorariums. Use the gifts to finance future puppet projects.

● ● ●

Starting a puppet team in your church requires a great deal of thought and prayer, and a willingness to commit your time and energy to a worthwhile cause. As you recruit others to join the puppet team, share your vision with them about the team's future and the possibilities for ministry. Then work together to make your puppet team all that it can be.

CHAPTER 3

The Puppet Family Tree

Now that you've recruited kids and adults for a puppet ministry team, you're ready to think about the tools of your new trade: puppets. People often assume that "puppets" refers to certain polyfoam creations similar to Jim Henson's Muppet family. But that's just one kind of puppet in the puppet family tree. Several other types can be used by your puppet team, depending on your interests, needs, audience and message.

Introducing the Family

Churches have used all of the six general puppet types in their ministries. Let's meet a representative from each limb of the puppet family tree.

Meet Shades. One of the oldest family members is the shadow puppet. An audience never sees Shades, but sees only the puppet's shadow. Puppeteers manipulate and move the puppet to simulate live action.

Shadow puppets can be cut from leather, heavy tagboard or "junk" materials such as plastic foam or cardboard. Moving parts can be added by connecting separate puppet pieces with wires.

Shadow puppets work by holding the puppets up between a strong light source—such as a 150-watt light—and a translucent screen. As the figure is held in front of the light, it casts a shadow on the screen. The audience sits on the other side of the screen and watches the shadow. The puppeteer can manipulate the figure across the screen with one hand while moving the parts with the other hand to get believable action of the character.

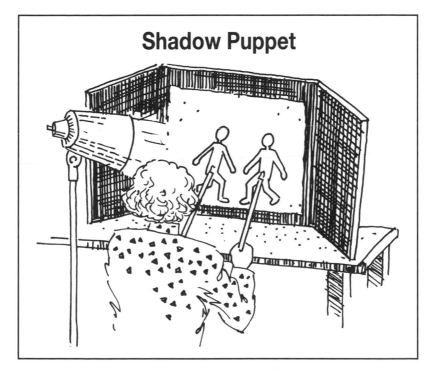

Shadow Puppet

Shadow puppets are very inexpensive and easy to manipulate. But sometimes they lack the sophistication needed to hold an audience's interest.

Meet Hands. This simple puppet consists of a puppet "head" made from plastic foam, papier-maché or some other material, and a cloth "body"—similar to a glove—that fits over a hand. This puppet is easy and inexpensive to make. All you need is paint, cloth, needle and thread, and something to make the head out of.

The puppet comes to life when an index finger is placed

in the puppet's head and the thumb and middle finger become the puppet's arms. It can pick up objects easily and express a wide range of emotions. However, it's relatively small and only works well with small audiences. Also, the absence of a moving mouth makes this puppet less desirable.

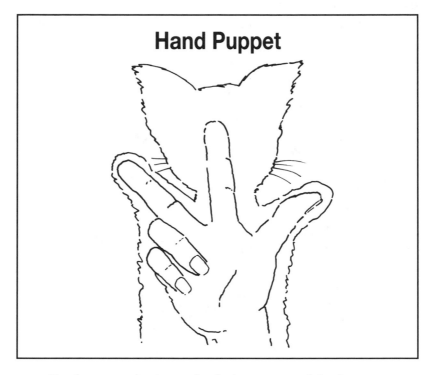

Hand Puppet

By the way, don't overlook the power of the human hand acting alone. With the movement and expressive capabilities of four fingers and a thumb, a human hand can communicate complex thoughts, ideas—even humor! The hand can don a white glove and present sign language under a black light. Two hands can also work together for the same effect.

In addition, a hand on either side of a stage might become a pair of "stage hands" bringing props, bowing after the work is done or clapping after the performance. Hands can also become walking creatures, meeting each other, expressing emotions or reacting to one another as puppets on stage. Creativity unlocks many doors for these expressive tools.

Meet Rod. The rod puppet consists of a puppet figure supported by a single stick or pole held from below. Other rods can be attached to arms or legs for gestures or additional movements.

Simple characters such as bees or butterflies lend themselves to this type of puppet. However, complicated puppets can also be constructed by adding strings or wires to additional moving parts. Often objects such as mops, brooms or yardsticks can become unique puppet characters through the addition of eyes, ears, mouths and other character parts.

Rod Puppet

Meet Mari. An action story with two or more characters moving in and out of the scene lends itself to the marionette style of puppetry. The entire puppet body is visible to the audience and a skilled puppeteer manipulates strings attached to the puppet to cause it to perform human-like movements.

Marionettes require a stage built especially for them. Hence, this type of puppet doesn't mix well with the other family members.

Marionette

Marionette manipulation requires great finger dexterity and practice, and is considered more difficult than other types of puppetry. Simple marionettes may be made and used by children, but the more advanced, complicated types require much more skill to make and manipulate.

Meet Vent-Pal. A popular puppet in the puppet family tree is the ventriloquist's partner—sometimes called a dummy. Humor is its trademark, and illusion is the key to its success. In ventriloquism, a puppeteer brings a puppet to life while he or she remains in full view of the audience. The puppeteer, or ventriloquist, must create a distinct character voice for his or her vent-pal, give the audience the illusion that the character is speaking totally on its own, focus his or her attention on the puppet, and avoid all lip movement and facial gestures while the puppet's talking.

Generally, a ventriloquist works with only one puppet at a time, some performers have mastered the voices and manipulation of two or even three characters simultaneously carrying on a conversation with the puppeteer.

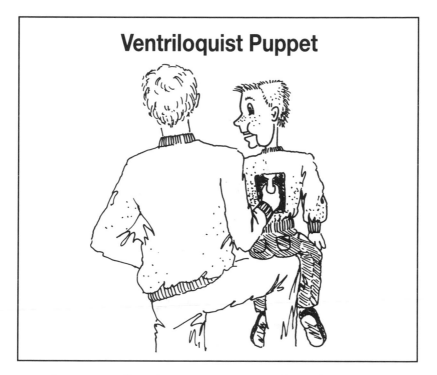

Ventriloquist Puppet

Some ventriloquist puppets are simple and inexpensive, but most are complicated and costly. Those with several moving facial parts have a complicated control stick that requires a great deal of physical dexterity. For more information on ventriloquism see Appendix B on page 125.

Meet Mouthy. In recent years, the moving-mouth hand puppet has become the most popular puppet type, owing much of its success to TV programs such as *Sesame Street* and *The Muppet Show.*

A moving-mouth hand puppet typically is a half-bodied puppet with stuffed arms made mobile by attaching a rod to each wrist. One of the puppeteer's hands fits into the mouth of the puppet, which opens once for each syllable spoken by the puppet. The puppeteer's other hand operates one or both rods attached to the arms in order to make the puppet more lifelike.

Because the mouth must be opened and closed for each syllable of each word, these puppets require more hand and arm strength and physical effort than any other type. They're also more difficult to construct than some types. However, this type of puppet can express a wide array of emotions and movements, which makes it ideal for many puppet teams.

Moving-Mouth Hand Puppet

A similar type puppet is the human arm moving-mouth puppet. This character uses the same style of mouth action, but instead of stuffed arms for manipulation by rods, the puppeteer puts his own arm into an extension of the puppet's sleeve, becoming one arm and hand of the puppet. The puppeteer wears a glove which matches the face of the puppet, creating the illusion that the puppet has mobile and lifelike hands. If both of the puppet's hands are needed in a performance, the puppet must be operated by two puppeteers—one operating the head, the other operating both hands.

Choosing Your Puppets

Before you spend time making puppets or investing in ready-made ones, decide which puppet type best fits your team's needs. Most puppet teams choose the moving-mouth hand puppets because of their versatility and durability. Also, kids can learn to manipulate these puppets more quickly than they could a marionette or a complicated rod puppet.

If you use moving-mouth hand puppets as the founda-

Buying and Sewing

Puppets are the centerpiece of your puppet ministry. Therefore, they need to be top-quality products. But that doesn't always mean lots of money. You can purchase ready-made puppets from a puppet supply company, or you can create them from patterns provided by puppet stores or members of your congregation. See the advantages and disadvantages of these options:

Buying

Advantages	Disadvantages
● You can usually get the puppets quickly.	● Puppets cost more initially.
● You'll get professional-quality puppets.	● Your puppets will look similar to other groups' puppets.
● They'll usually last longer than hand-made puppets.	● You must plan your skits in time to get the puppets you'll need.
● You can see what you're getting.	● Sometimes ready-made puppets are stiff and difficult to manipulate.

Sewing

Advantages	Disadvantages
● Puppets cost less.	● You must find a good pattern with clear directions.
● You can create unique characters.	● It usually takes more time.
● You can personalize your puppets.	● It often takes several attempts to create a quality puppet.
● You have total control over costuming, skin color, size and type.	● Materials are sometimes hard to find.

Whatever puppets you choose, make sure they're worthy of representing your church and the purpose of your ministry. Don't use any puppets your puppeteers are ashamed to be seen with!

tion of your puppet ensemble, include a few shadow puppets or rod puppets to add variety to your program and give your puppeteers an added challenge.

In the beginning, choose moving-mouth hand puppets that are the most usable with a variety of scripts and songs. For example, a boy moving-mouth hand puppet can be costumed as a grandpa or a biblical character. But a bird or dog puppet can't be used for anything other than what it is. Use animal characters as emcees, storytellers or in other special roles.

Some puppet characters are designed so that the eyes, nose, ears, and hair can be removed and reattached with Velcro. This seems great until you remember that any feature that's removable is also losable! Still, you may want puppets with removable clothing and hair so they can easily take on other roles.

Caring for Your Tools

In puppet ministry, your puppets and props are your tools. And whether you've purchased your puppets or made them, they represent a sizable investment of time and money. Because of this, special care must be taken to store and transport puppets to keep them in good condition.

Since most puppets are made of fabric and foam, they can become soiled or damaged unless cared for properly. When puppets are new, spray them with a fabric protector. If you get a dirty spot or stain on the puppet, surface wash the soiled area with a mild spot remover or fabric cleaner.

Puppeteers must be carefully trained to take care of the puppets. Here are some Dos and Don'ts to help you lengthen your puppets' lives.

Do	**Don't**
● Store puppets in a box or trunk away from dust, dampness or unsupervised children.	● Leave puppets lying around on the floor where people will step on them.
● When packing puppets into boxes, remove the rods. Place	● Pack puppets too tightly. That will smash the puppets.

puppets with faces toward the inside, away from the box surface.

● Treat puppets as if they're very fragile—they are!

● Brush a puppet's hair before each entrance.

● Check the positioning of the foam inside each puppet's body before it enters the performance stage.

● Pick puppets up by the hair, nose or ears—ouch!

● Bite *anything* with the mouth of a puppet. Doing so will bend, break and eventually ruin the cardboard stiffener in the puppet's mouth.

● Allow puppeteers to bang puppets together.

● Allow puppeteers to eat or drink while working with puppets. Greasy hands and spilled drinks are dangerous to your puppets' health.

Now that you've met all the members of the puppet family tree and know how to care for your puppets, you're ready to focus on effective puppet manipulation techniques. We'll concentrate our efforts on the moving-mouth hand puppet since that's the most common type of puppet used in puppet ministry. However, the ideas presented will be helpful for any style of puppetry your ministry may tackle.

Emergency! Emergency!

When a doctor goes on a house call, he takes every tool or instrument he might need. When a plumber comes to fix your plumbing, he brings the tools he needs to complete the job.

So it makes sense that a puppet team carry a "tool" box to every practice and performance to take care of minor emergencies without wasting time and energy.

Many teams use a fishing tackle box or carpenter's tool box because of the many little storage compartments.

Use this checklist when stocking your puppet team's tool box:

❑ contact cement

❑ small hammer

❑ X-ACTO knife

❑ duct tape

❑ razor blades

❑ extension cords

❑ hand lotion

❑ matches

❑ stapler

❑ safety pins

❑ spare gloves for human-hand puppets

❑ pliers

❑ scissors

❑ ruler

❑ scotch tape

❑ screwdrivers (Phillips and regular)

❑ thumbtacks

❑ straight pins

❑ black magic marker

❑ rubber bands

❑ spare eyes for puppets

❑ three-prong plug adapters

In addition to these items, carry business cards or copies of a small brochure about your puppet ministry. If you do a sharp program, you'll have people from the audience wanting to book you for an engagement at their church or organization.

CHAPTER 4

Bringing Puppets to Life

A good puppeteer can make a foam and fabric object become a believable, attention-getting character. The puppet is an actor, and the puppeteer controls the actor's movements.

But making a puppet come to life on stage isn't easy. The skills puppeteers need to project a character through a puppet require time, practice and, most of all, attention to detail. Puppeteers need to learn the techniques "right the first time" so the skills they need will eventually come naturally.

Standing in the Spotlight

A puppet's movements and position are critical to the success of the character you're portraying. Examine these basic puppet manipulation techniques each of your puppeteers must learn.

Entering and exiting—You want the puppet to appear to walk into and out of view. To accomplish this, face the front of the stage, reach back behind your head and "walk" the puppet up four or five imaginary stairs toward the stage. From the audience's view, the puppet is walking toward the front of the stage and "up the stairs" into full view.

To exit, just reverse the procedure, turning the puppet's back to the stage and walking it down and away from the audience in the same stair-step motion.

While your moving-mouth hand puppet is on stage, your arm should be extended straight up from your shoulder. Don't bend your elbow except during the entrance and exit. If you attempt to perform with a bent elbow, your puppet's height will vary greatly and your arm will tire quickly.

Positioning—After the puppet has entered into view of the audience, the audience shouldn't see the puppeteer's arm. Nor should people see just the puppet's head. The proper height is "belly button level"—if the puppet had a belly button, it would be even with the top of the stage.

Also, keep the puppet at least eight inches back from the stage to allow room for arm movements and other actions.

Lip synchronization—The moving-mouth hand puppet requires precise manipulation to make the mouth movement seem realistic. In general, open the puppet's mouth once for each syllable of spoken words, and close it between the syllables or when the puppet isn't talking.

For example, to say "hello," open the puppet's mouth twice. To say "My name is Bobby," open the puppet's mouth five times—once for each syllable.

When making a puppet speak, a beginning puppeteer will commonly "flip the lid" of the puppet, or move the top part of the puppet's head for each syllable. This makes the puppet throw its head back every time it speaks. With practice, though, any puppeteer can learn to lower the puppet's jaw instead of flip its lid. That way the puppet maintains proper eye contact with the audience.

Another common error is to open the puppet's mouth as wide as possible every time it speaks. If the puppet is whispering or speaking softly, open the mouth just a little. If the puppet is talking normally, open the mouth one-third to one-half way. If the puppet is yawning, yelling or singing loudly, open the mouth to its fullest extent.

Making All the Right Moves

When the puppets are "standing" at the correct height on stage, maintaining eye contact with the audience and even moving their mouths in sync with the tape, the learning has just begun. Puppeteers must still learn to make all the puppets' movements believable.

Rod-arm-puppet movements—Attaching a rod to one of the puppet's arms greatly increases the range of movement possible for that puppet. Attach the rod to the puppet's left wrist if the puppeteer is right-handed, or vice versa. Then practice using the puppet's arm to express these actions:

- Scratch its head.
- Throw kisses.
- Take a bow.
- Cough.
- Express sadness.
- Show excitement.
- Rub its tummy.
- Yawn.
- Sneeze.
- Do a double take.
- Express fear.
- Rub its eyes.
- Look into the distance.
- Show concentration.
- Pretend to be hard of hearing.

Once you've mastered lip sync with one rod attached, try two-handed movements with rods attached to both arms. But keep in mind that not all movements require both arms. When using two rods together, cross them in an "X," holding the top of the two rods between your thumb and index finger while slipping your little finger between the rods at the bottom of the X. See the illustration on page 34.

Now experiment with the following two-rod moves:

- Clap hands.
- Fly like an airplane.
- Blow nose.
- Pray.
- Sneeze.
- Do jumping jacks.
- Play peekaboo.
- Run in place.
- Have a coughing fit.

Human-arm puppet movements—Human-arm puppets require cooperation between two puppeteers. The puppeteers' positioning is awkward and requires stamina. Use these procedures when training puppeteers to operate a two-handed human-arm puppet.

- One puppeteer operates the head, while the other puppeteer operates both the puppet's hands.
- The taller puppeteer operates the head.
- The "head" operator stands behind the "hands" operator.
- The hands operator kneels on both knees. The head operator kneels on one knee between the legs of the hands operator.

● The puppet's body stays 10 to 12 inches away from the stage to give the hands room to operate.

● The hands always drop out of sight before the puppet moves from one location to another.

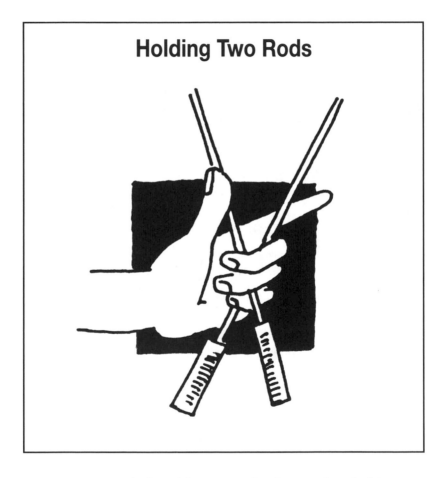

Holding Two Rods

To practice believable actions for the one-handed human-arm puppet, use the list of actions for the single-rod-arm puppet. For the two-handed human-arm puppet, try these movements:

● Read a Bible.
● Sit down and think.
● Clap.

● Direct a song.
● Bite fingernails.
● Run in place.

● Cover face.
● Blow nose.
● Throw paper wads.

Dressing the Part

Some say "clothes make the man," and it's certainly true that costuming can work wonders in helping your puppets come alive! Use these suggestions to improve your puppetry through costuming.

Collect hats. Use cowboy hats, Jewish skullcaps, turbans, women's hats, Chinese hats, Indian feathers or headdresses, police hats, firefighter hats, construction worker hats, baseball hats, visors—any hats that convey certain characters or moods. Find them in secondhand stores or toy shops. Also, Halloween is an excellent time to pick up unique hats and other costume items.

Collect toddlers' clothes. The best puppetry costuming can often be found in your neighbor's garage. Sizes 2 to 4 work best. Also collect cloth scraps to use as puppet accessories, such as scarves or headbands.

When using costumes or other props, make sure they are securely attached to the puppet. Nothing damages a puppet play as much as costuming falling off or flopping around. Avoid this by sewing costuming directly on the puppets. Or use safety pins or Velcro.

Creating Character Through Voice

So your puppet looks good and moves in a convincing manner. But what happens when your puppet must speak?

Puppets are fantasy figures. They look similar to cartoons. And their voices should reflect what they are. Puppet voices should appeal to the audience and be easily understood. But they should also have a cartoon-character quality. Puppet voices can be categorized into six basic voice qualities:

1. Whispered—Use your own voice but add a strong whisper over it at all times.

2. Nasal—Exaggerate the "n" sound behind all your words, squeezing the air through your nose as you talk.

3. Goofy—Drop the pitch, slow the tempo and move into the mind-set of "Duh, I dunno."

4. Guttural—Use a rolling "r" behind all your words to convey harshness or to make animal sounds such as a dog's growl or a lion's roar.

5. Falsetto—Talk about an octave above your regular pitch.

6. Melodic—Almost sing the words and add a rich vibrato. Give your words an operatic feel.

You can create scores of characters from these six basic voices by experimenting with other elements of sound.

● Pitch—how high or low the tone of the voice sounds. For example, a little girl would have a high voice, while a football player would have a low voice.

● Volume—how soft or loud a character speaks. For example, a country farmer might speak loudly, while a shy boy might speak quietly.

● Tempo—how fast or slow the character speaks. For example, a mouse character might rattle words off quickly, while a turtle would speak slowly.

● Diction—how a word is pronounced. For example, a city puppet might pronounce nothing "no-thing," but a rural puppet might say "nut-tin."

● Word choice—how words are chosen to fit the character you're creating. For example, a grandpa puppet might say "young-uns," while a child puppet might say "kids."

● ● ●

Encourage your puppeteers to be patient as they learn correct puppet-manipulation techniques. Have kids practice them every time you rehearse. Taking time to learn these techniques in the early stages of your puppet ministry will save you time and quality later. And good skills, when combined with creative costuming and fun voice effects, will heighten puppeteers' enjoyment and increase your ministry's effectiveness.

CHAPTER 5

Designing a Program

When architects design a building, they always consider the area's climate. A building built in Anchorage, Alaska, for instance, would be quite different from one in Key West, Florida.

Planning performance material works much the same way. The material you select needs to fit the "climate"—or audience. Puppets can be used effectively with all types of audiences. Teenagers, elementary kids, adults, preschoolers and senior citizens can all join in the fun of puppetry.

Puppetry can also be done in different settings, such as public parks, malls, hospitals, even prisons.

With properly chosen material, puppetry can entertain and inspire people in any of these audiences or settings. Let's consider how puppetry could be used effectively in each of these audiences and settings.

Preschoolers—Young children have a short attention span, so avoid any play that's more than three minutes long. Songs should also be short and familiar so children can sing along. Use several different puppets throughout the performance and have the puppets interact with the kids as much as possible.

Elementary kids—Children are always an eager audience for puppet songs and skits. Current Christian musicals for children can often be done with puppets. Skits should be kept short, lasting no longer than five minutes.

Puppet plays can consist of Bible stories, modern adaptations of Bible stories or topical skits with a biblical message kids can understand.

One technique that works well with children is to use a real person—such as one of the puppeteers—in front of the stage to interact with a puppet. This helps maintain audience control and attention.

Teenagers—Young people like puppets for the same reasons other people do: They're fun, they remind us of childhood and they entertain us with their often wild antics.

Teenagers almost always enjoy puppets, but especially when they do skits that deal with teenage issues or relationships. Use material that contains teenage lingo or parodies of popular teenage idols. Rewrite Bible stories using modern characters and situations, getting the same truth across.

Also, skits focusing on family problems can be effective. For example, act out a tense conflict between a father and son, then interview each character individually to get his side of the story. From there, launch a discussion with the audience, having them suggest possible resolutions. You might want to have the puppets act out the audience's suggestions.

Adults—Adults enjoy takeoffs on current TV shows, well-known personalities or popular songs. Material for adults should contain humor yet effectively hit on issues adults deal with daily. With puppets you can tackle touchy subjects—like giving, honesty and church participation—much easier than a pastor can.

Senior citizens—This audience prefers relatively slow, familiar, easy-to-understand songs. They'll also enjoy the children's songs they sang as kids.

Use grandpa and grandma puppet characters to talk about Bible stories or the more recent past. Allow the audience to interact with the puppets—have puppets tell jokes, ask questions or just reminisce with the audience.

Public parks and malls—People in these settings are usually on their way somewhere and have little time to spare. Therefore, design a clever, action-packed program that'll grab their attention. Keep segments short, to the point and suitable for adults as well as children. Lively puppet songs coupled with a capable "out front" person work well in this situation. Remember to secure permission from the mall manager or park supervisor and follow the facility's guidelines.

Hospitals and prisons—These audiences each are unique, so take special care to talk to a representative of the institution about the type of audience you're dealing with. Discuss your performance segments to be certain the things you choose to perform are appropriate.

Put yourself in the audience's place and evaluate your material as if you were one of them. Be sensitive to the special needs and background of each person in your audience.

Choosing Your Material

No matter who your audience is, you'll want material with a message. However, you'll also want some "just for fun" material to provide comic relief and add interest to the program.

Guidelines for developing a program differ depending on whether you're performing live or from a tape, as well as whether you want a musical or a drama. Let's look at each of these options.

Live material—For live performances, stick with skits that have only two or three characters and are less than five minutes long. Long, live productions can be tiresome—both for the puppeteers and the audience. Cut longer programs into several three- to five-minute segments, with fun narratives or vignettes between.

When choosing skits to perform as live material, ask yourself these questions:

● Do we have kids who can project their voices effectively?

● Do we have kids who can create voices to match the characters in the skit?

● Do we have enough puppeteers to do all the voices or will some puppeteers have to do more than one voice?

● Does the skit have any hard-to-memorize speeches?

Your Performance Style

A major consideration in puppet ministry is deciding whether to perform live or with taped material. There are many advantages to each approach. Let's take a look at a few of them.

Advantages of Live Material
- You can tailor your program to a specific audience more easily.
- You can interact with the audience more easily.
- You can react to unexpected problems or audience response.
- You don't have to bother with tape equipment.

Disadvantages of Live Material
- The puppeteer must work with a microphone.
- The puppeteer must change his or her voice for different characters, and speak clearly and distinctly.
- Live songs usually don't work as well as prerecorded ones.

Advantages of Taped Material
- An abundance of puppet songs and skits are available.
- You can use music and sound effects you can't do live.
- The result sounds more professional.
- You can have special voices your puppeteers may not be able to do.

Disadvantages of Taped Material
- The tape can break or be "eaten" by the tape player.
- Sometimes the program sounds canned.
- More rehearsal time is needed to memorize the tape's timing.
- Taped performing prevents interaction with the audience.

Taped material—Choose taped skits that sound professional, yet not "canned." Also, consider the skit's message and story line to determine what audiences you could use it with. Avoid skits that have only limited usefulness. For example, a Christmas skit aimed at senior citizens can likely be used only once or twice before it becomes old.

When choosing prerecorded puppet skits, ask yourself these questions:

- Are the words intelligible?
- Are the lines short, concise and not "preachy"?
- Are there only two or three characters on stage at a time?
- Are extravagant sets and props required?
- Is there enough time for entrances, exits and scene changes?

● Is any one character on stage for more than five minutes at a time?

Programming for One

In addition to programs designed for entire puppet teams, you can also "go solo" with puppets, using them to interact with groups or just to entertain. Check out these three ideas for using puppets to help you lead or interact with your group:

Puppet specials—Select a song that fits the theme of an upcoming meeting. Then send a puppet and cassette tape of the song home with an interested teenager. Ask him or her to practice the song and be ready to perform it for the group on the appropriate week. Don't worry if the puppetry isn't perfect—kids will enjoy seeing a peer make the attempt.

Story time—Use a puppet character to tell stories that relate to the meeting theme each week. Make the stories silly and lighthearted. Kids may laugh and joke about "that crazy youth minister and that goofy puppet," but don't let that discourage you. The story's message will still get through.

Drama mops—For a twist on storytelling time, give some of the kids mops and brooms, and have them create rod puppets. Encourage kids to use anything they can find—paper, cloth, wire or whatever—to create faces and costumes for the mops and brooms.

Have kids with puppets kneel behind a partition in front of the class. Tell a story and have puppeteers act it out as you speak. This is great fun for the kids and provides a creative way to get your point across.

Puppet songs—When choosing songs for your puppets to sing, consider these suggestions:

● Match the number of voices on the tape to the number of puppets you use. Avoid the "choir" sound whenever possible.

● Make sure the audience will be able to understand the words.

● Choose lively songs. The greatest puppeteers in the world would have trouble keeping an audience awake if the songs put them to sleep.

● Pick songs that have a purpose. This doesn't necessarily mean a spiritual message. Perhaps you want the song to entertain or to make the audience laugh. That's okay. What's important is that the song has a specific, positive effect on the audience.

● Choose songs that can be choreographed. Think of how costuming, props or special effects could enhance the song's message.

● Match the type of song with the puppets you're using. For example, a black gospel ballad won't work well if you have only white puppets.

Complete musical productions—Several complete musicals have been written for puppets. They're similar to choir musicals, but include stage directions and characters better fitted to puppet ministry. Productions like these work well for puppet teams that go on tour or perform the same production many times in their area.

When considering a full-length musical production with puppets, consider these questions:

● Can the puppet team physically handle a 30- to 40-minute presentation?

● Is this musical's spiritual message worth your effort, time and expense?

● Do the musical styles vary or do all the songs sound the same?

● Is there a meaningful story line between the songs?

● Does the musical require certain characters to stay on stage for long periods? If so, would it be possible to switch puppeteers to provide a rest for overworked arms?

● Could the youth choir or children's choir sing the songs and have the puppets do only the drama segments?

Putting It All Together

After you've learned the basics of puppet manipulation, selected songs and skits to work on, and have a few practices behind you, it won't be long before you're called on to perform.

Don't panic! Putting a program together really isn't all that hard. Begin by answering these two questions:

1. What type of audience is it?
2. How long does the program need to be?

Once you answer these two questions, scan the skits and songs you've worked on and decide whether any are appropriate for this performance.

If so, you're in good shape. If not, ask yourself if you have enough time to prepare new material. If not, turn down the invitation—instead of performing inappropriate material or poorly rehearsed songs and skits.

If you do have time to prepare a new program, where do you begin? Here are some steps to take.

Develop a theme. Whatever audience or program length you have, you need a theme for your presentation. A theme can focus on a Bible verse, a biblical truth such as forgiveness, a virtue such as honesty, or a relational issue such as making friends or getting along with Mom and Dad. Holiday themes also work well if the timing is right.

Tie the segments together. A puppet presentation usually contains several segments, such as recorded puppet songs, live Bible verses, live or recorded puppet skits and puppet interaction with the audience. Each of these segments must fit together smoothly with an effective transition or "bridge." One of the best ways to build this bridge is with a narrator puppet that carries the audience from one scene to the next. The narrator tells a story, sings a song, interacts with the audience or just explains what's coming up next.

Using a "bridge" character has two advantages:

● It gives the puppeteers time to switch positions backstage and to change or dress puppets.

● It provides a way to connect the segments to your theme.

Even if your collection of skits and songs seems disjointed, you can usually pull it together around a theme by using a bridge character throughout the program.

Get feedback. When you perform, always ask your host what he or she thought of the program. Try to get honest criticism. Also, ask puppeteers to express their feelings about their performance. Ask them how things are going backstage and what changes or improvements can be made.

Burn Out or Rust Out

Once your puppet ministry is in operation, your team will need to determine how often to perform. If you perform too often—especially the same material over and over—your team members may start to show signs of burnout.

On the other hand, if you practice and practice but never perform, your team may grow restless and discouraged. That condition is often called rustout. And you can correct it only by getting your team in front of an audience more often.

So how often should you perform? No one answer applies to everyone. Some teams perform once or twice a week—and like it that way. Other teams perform once or twice a month. And some spend two or three months rehearsing a full-length musical, then perform several times in a matter of days.

You'll need to determine the correct spacing of performances for your group. Several factors may affect your performance schedule, such as team members' personal schedules, availability of transportation and the number of people who can help with putting on a production. Consider these prayerfully as you set the calendar for your puppet team.

● ● ●

Putting together a program for your puppet team can be a fun, rewarding experience. But it also takes time, energy and a knack for knowing just what skits or songs will fit a particular audience. It also takes skill to make a variety of skits and songs flow together smoothly as one unified program.

But don't let that discourage you. With a little practice and some positive experiences, you'll soon grow confident of your ability to effectively convey a message through puppets.

CHAPTER 6

Practice Makes Perfect

A puppet ministry team, in many ways, is like a drama group. Participants memorize scripts and movements, develop muscular abilities and learn to work together as a team.

And that takes practice.

Teams need regular rehearsals to develop the muscular strength, memorization skills and cooperation needed to master the plays, skits and songs of puppet ministry. Most puppet teams find meeting for an hour and a half each week is about right.

Successful rehearsals focus on three areas: devotions, communication and practice. Dividing your puppet rehearsals this way gives you the practice time you need, while not ignoring team members' spiritual growth or relationships. Let's look more closely at each of these areas.

Devotions—Spend the first 15 to 30 minutes of each rehearsal doing an active devotion with the kids. Encourage kids to talk about their concerns, personal needs and victories. One good resource to use for devotion ideas is *10-Minute Devotions for Youth Groups* by J.B. Collingsworth (Group Books). The book contains 52 easy-to-use devotions on issues that concern kids.

Allow puppeteers to take turns leading the devotion time. Also, invite parents to lead a devotion from time to time.

Keep the devotions fresh and active. Don't let kids think of it as "down time"—time when they sit quietly and shut off their brains. Instead, play games that teach a lesson or have kids interact with each other.

See the "Where Ministry Begins" box below for more insights on ministry with puppeteers.

Where Ministry Begins

Since your puppet team is a ministry, develop a ministry attitude in your rehearsal time together. Consider these suggestions for helping kids focus on ministry in puppetry.
- Never allow puppeteers to ridicule or put each other down.
- Have puppeteers choose prayer partners, and give them time in rehearsal to share personal concerns and pray for each other.
- Allow puppeteers to perform puppet songs they like, and spend time discussing the songs' words and meanings.
- Stress that your team's purpose is to serve others. Encourage puppeteers to serve each other by working together backstage, assisting each other whenever possible.
- Invite your pastor or other staff members to interact with your puppeteers and talk about what they think ministry is all about.

Communication time—As the director, you must regularly communicate details of upcoming performances and allow kids to ask questions or express concerns. Encourage kids each to bring a calendar to mark performance dates. Allow about 10 to 15 minutes to discuss upcoming performances and to field kids' questions. Also mail a performance and practice schedule to puppeteers' parents so they'll know what to expect.

Practice time—Spend about one-third of the rehearsal time working on basic techniques, such as entering and exiting, lip sync, rod-arm use and maintaining proper height. Use the remaining time developing your repertoire of songs and skits for performances. Practice a variety of skits—funny, serious, musical, action-packed, reflective—to keep puppeteers' interest.

Effective Policies

Before diving into a full-blown rehearsal schedule, discuss your team's purposes and goals with your team members, and set up policies to help you reach those goals. Write all the team's policies—concerning attendance, behavior and church participation—and have team members each sign and date it. Make sure they understand what's expected of them.

The toughest issue you'll deal with may be regulating rehearsal attendance and absences. Since every puppeteer will have assigned parts, it's vital that you develop a fairly strict attendance policy so rehearsal time stays productive. On the other hand, school assignments, family demands and unexpected occurrences require some flexibility.

Other areas may also require policy statements. For example, many teenagers have time conflicts between jobs and rehearsals. Think about possible problems you'll encounter, and develop policies to deal with these problems before they occur.

See the "Sample Policy Statement" on page 48 for more ideas.

Productive Planning

Rehearsal time can be fun, productive and enjoyable—provided you plan your time effectively. Here are 12 hints for making rehearsal time work for rather than against you.

1. Hold regular rehearsals. Set a regular time to practice each week and don't change it unless absolutely necessary.

2. Arrive early. Be there at least 30 minutes before rehearsal time to get everything organized: puppets, props, rods, tapes, tape players, scripts, devotions and anything else you'll need. Maybe ask a different puppeteer to help you prepare each week.

3. Write your rehearsal agenda. Prepare a schedule of what you want the team to rehearse, as well as a listing of required puppets, tapes, scripts, props and assigned parts. This will help you keep on track during rehearsal.

Sample Policy Statement

First Church of Somewhere, U.S.A.
Mr. and Mrs. Puppet Leader, Directors

1. The puppet team will meet in the sanctuary from 7 to 8:30 p.m. every Tuesday. All puppeteers are required to be on time.

2. Any puppeteer who has to miss a rehearsal or performance *for any reason* must notify the puppet director as far in advance as possible. Failure to notify the puppet director in advance of any absence may result in temporary suspension from the team.

3. Puppeteers *may not* bring visitors to rehearsals without prior permission of the director.

4. Puppeteers may not bring radios, electronic games, tape players or other distractions to rehearsals.

5. Excessive absence from puppet practice will result in suspension from the team.

6. Puppeteers may bring homework to rehearsals, but must put it away when asked to do so. The puppet directors will help puppeteers with homework as needed after the rehearsal is over.

7. Puppeteers will take an active role in deciding on material the team will perform and where the team will perform it.

8. All puppeteers are expected to attend services at First Church regularly. Each puppeteer must attend at least four church services or activities per month in addition to puppet rehearsals.

9. Puppeteers may earn personal credit through participation in fund-raising activities and by performing in extra "paid" performances. This credit remains in the puppetry fund, and can be used *only* toward the annual puppetry tour.

Team Verse
Ecclesiastes 9:10a—"Whatever your hand finds to do, do it with all your might."

4. Keep everyone busy. If your puppeteers sit around all evening, they'll wonder why they're there. If you have too many people to manage, get more help. One leader can work best with five to eight puppeteers at a time. Have alternative activities ready for puppeteers who aren't directly involved in the skit you're rehearsing. Have them help make costumes, clean puppets or practice new voices.

5. Don't get into a rut. Include something new each week. Let kids hear or try out new material. Spend time working on new live voices. Have kids switch parts. Have a party. Watch a video. Go out for fast food—anything to keep rehearsals exciting!

Experiment with these suggestions to avoid the "rehearsal rut."

● Have a Puppet Raid! Take your team to someone's house and do an impromptu skit. You could even show up with all your puppets on your pastor's front porch.

● Have a Puppet Visitation Night, where your puppeteers go to a visitor's house and have the puppets invite that person back to church.

● Have a Puppet Polaroid Scavenger Hunt. Divide your team into groups of two to four, give each team an instant-print camera and a puppet. Give kids a list of places to take a picture of their puppet; for example, behind the wheel of a police car, under a hair dryer or peeking out of a dumpster. But warn kids to keep their puppets clean wherever they go.

● Plan a Puppet Shopping Spree. Take your puppets to a discount store, and let them try on shirts, hats or other clothing items. Then purchase the items for your prop box and puppet wardrobe.

6. Allow time to learn material. Don't do a 40-minute musical after only two or three rehearsals. After kids learn to lip-sync songs or plays, they still must work on staging, choreography, props and other extras that make the production unique.

7. Direct from the audience's perspective. Stand in front of the stage as you direct. Avoid performing unless absolutely necessary. You need to be the "eyes of the audience," and deal with problems in positioning, puppet manipulation and height during the rehearsal.

8. Emphasize positive things you see. Puppeteers need positive reinforcement as well as constructive criticism. Point out the good things you see happening—avoid just pointing out kids' errors.

9. Encourage puppeteers to learn all the parts. You never know when illness or an unexpected absence may require you to switch puppeteers' parts. Encourage puppeteers to pay attention to every part in case changes must be made.

10. Practice a variety of material. Rehearse a broad spectrum of material: comic and serious; musical and dramatic; taped and live; seasonal and non-seasonal. Not only does it keep rehearsals interesting, it also challenges kids to stretch their puppeteering abilities.

11. Take time for fun! Plan parties, trips and other fun times. Reward puppeteers for their work and dedication. Sometimes an ice cream cone says much more than a thousand "thank yous."

12. Delegate responsibility to puppeteers. Kids can do most of the tasks in puppet ministry, such as setting up the stage, gathering puppets and props, grooming puppets and putting away equipment after rehearsal.

Successful Scheduling

It takes experience to know how much time to rehearse a skit before you perform it. Spending too much time on one piece makes puppetry boring, while not spending enough time can discourage puppeteers. The following steps apply to learning prerecorded material. Learning live material follows a similar path, with time added for script reading and voice development.

1. Review the material with puppeteers. Answer questions such as: "What are we doing?" "Why are we doing it?" and "Where will we use it?" Puppeteers need to understand why they're doing a particular piece and how it'll be used in ministry.

2. Play the tape. Have puppeteers read the script as they listen.

3. Assign parts to puppeteers. Normally you should decide who should take each part, based on each puppeteer's skill, voice and present workload.

4. Play the tape again. Have puppeteers move their thumbs in sync with the voices on the tape.

5. Have puppeteers listen to the tape and lip-sync with their puppets. After a few practice runs, have puppeteers put away their scripts and just follow the tape.

Puppetry Skill Levels

Motivating kids isn't easy. And puppetry requires the kind of long-term dedication that only select teenagers have to give. But you can encourage kids' interest in puppet ministry and keep them striving to do better.

Here's a four-level achievement program to challenge your puppeteers toward excellence in puppetry. Puppeteers must fulfill the requirements listed to achieve each level.

Level One—Apprentice Puppeteer
● Attend puppet rehearsals regularly for three months.
● Learn basic puppet manipulation techniques.
● Learn to set up stages and care for the equipment.
● Maintain a good attitude toward leaders and other puppeteers.
● Participate in six performances, two of which must be away from the church.

Level Two—Journeyman Puppeteer
● Complete apprentice program.
● Attend puppet rehearsals regularly for one year.
● Participate in 10 performances, four of which must be away from the church.
● Participate in at least one puppet tour.

Level Three—Advanced Puppeteer
● Complete journeyman program.
● Attend puppet rehearsals regularly for two years.
● Show progress in performance skills, including use of two rods, human-hand techniques and live performance.
● Participate in at least two puppet tours.
● Successfully perform a lead role in one play or musical production.

Level Four—Master Puppeteer
● Complete advanced program.
● Attend puppet rehearsals regularly for three years.
● Be able to use at least three different "voices" in live performance.
● Write and perform a live puppet monologue or dialogue.
● Plan and direct one complete puppet rehearsal.

Award puppeteers different patches for each skill level. Encourage them to sew their patches to their puppetry shirts or jackets.

6. Move to the puppet stage. Have puppeteers work on positioning and on polishing their presentation. Go through the script several times, each time working out more details of movement and presentation.

7. Add props, scenery and costumes. Practice with everything in place until each puppeteer feels comfortable with his or her part. Then you're ready to perform!

Steps one through four could be accomplished in your team's first exposure to the material, steps five and six during the second and third rehearsals, and step seven can wait until the fourth rehearsal.

Each group's learning rate will be different, so you'll need to adjust the learning schedule to fit your team. Experience will tell you what works best for your puppet team.

● ● ●

Rehearsals are the foundation of your ministry with your team members. In rehearsals, not only do puppeteers learn their parts and develop their puppetry skills, they also interact with each other as members of a team. They learn to work through problems they have with other team members. And they discover the joy of "family" with other team members.

So make your team's rehearsals fun and meaningful. And provide ways for kids to grow through their relationships with each other.

CHAPTER 7

Write On!

John's puppet team has been asked to do a program for a teenage juvenile home. John and his team want to take advantage of this opportunity, but they can't find any scripts to fit the occasion. And John has never written a puppet script before.

But ...

John is great with puppets. His creativity shines every time he picks one up. He and his team members enjoy creating spontaneous conversations between their puppet characters.

John is a perfect candidate for writing his own puppet scripts.

● ● ●

Sooner or later in puppet ministry, the time will come when you can't find a suitable script for a specific need. Rather than miss an opportunity for ministry, why not write your own skit or play? Don't worry if you've never written anything before or if you don't feel you're creative enough. All it takes is time, brainstorming and guidance.

Follow the simple steps outlined in this chapter, and soon you'll be writing scripts and plays for all occasions.

Finding Your Inspiration

John decided to give scriptwriting a try. But where will he find ideas for topics, settings and characters? What if he can't come up with any hot ideas?

● ● ●

Some say there's no such thing as a new idea. In a way that's true, since our every thought is influenced by the billions of bits of information we've accumulated over the years.

So when you're looking for fresh ideas, don't feel bad about borrowing from others. Although you shouldn't use others' stories directly, you can borrow general concepts or ideas for use in a puppet drama. Creativity breeds creativity. So let others' creativity inspire your own ideas.

For starters, check out these resources.

Teenage magazines and books—Visit a Christian bookstore and browse through the magazine and book titles. Look for hot teenage topics or fads. You can also incorporate the latest teenage pop idols into your puppet scripts.

Teenage comedy albums and videos—Listen to comedians who work with teenagers and consider ways of adapting their style, ideas and methods to puppets.

TV shows—Many excellent puppet plays use familiar TV shows to convey biblical truth. For example, build a script around *The Tonight Show* with an emcee, co-host and lots of guests. In addition, programs like *The Wonder Years*—with its simple family humor—lend themselves to fun puppet skits using clever names and conflicts that bring out biblical truth.

Small group brainstorming—Get a group of teenagers together and brainstorm ideas for puppet characters, musical productions and script topics your group would enjoy. Kids have lots of ideas!

Bible stories—The Bible is filled with exciting stories that can make great puppet scripts. Outline the story details and make a list of all essential characters. Keep the story short and concise. For starters, adapt Jesus' parables or the story of David and Goliath.

John considered these options and decided to concentrate on TV shows and popular TV personalities—an area most teenagers can relate to. He began to scan the popular TV shows to see what or who jumped out at him. And he listened for topics covered in the shows that he might also want to cover in his production.

Developing Your Style

Skits can take on several different styles. A skit conveying the power of God, for example, can be done with humor, serious narration, songs or even no words at all. For each skit you produce, you must decide which style will most effectively get the message across.

The possibilities are endless. Consider these examples:

● serious—contemporary characters in real-life situations;

● fantasy—fantasy characters such as talking mushrooms, or unusual settings such as outer space or the ocean bottom;

● melodrama—hero and villain characters in an exaggerated style of good vs. evil;

● parable—characters acting out a parable from scripture;

● time change—characters set in the past or in the future;

● multicultural—each character's appearance, conversation and costuming reflect a specific cultural background, such as a cowboy, a Hispanic, an Eskimo or a Swede;

● TV takeoff—story patterned after characters or format of a popular TV program; and

● pantomime—characters act out a story without words.

Style your skits to highlight the truths you want to convey. For example, a skit about materialism might work well in a TV game show format. Or a skit about communication might be interesting done as a pantomime. Use your imagination and try new ways to convey truths to your audience.

After John investigated many of these sources, he decided on a variety program using a Bill Cosby puppet character named Dill Crosby as the emcee. The variety program, John decided, should contain a series of short, active skits that use humor to make a point. John opted to design each skit around a different TV show, so kids would readily recognize the characters and involve themselves in the skit's message.

Choosing Your Character

John had decided to use Bill Cosby as his model for the puppet emcee. But John had never imitated Bill Cosby. Fortunately, one of John's puppeteers was excellent at imitating people's voices. But there's much more to a character than just a voice, right?

Right. Character development is crucial to a successful script. The most poignant message in the world will never reach the audience if the characters aren't believable.

The first question any scriptwriter must ask is "How many characters should I use?" The answer is always "As few as possible!" Why? It's much easier to write and stage for one, two or three characters than for larger numbers. And the more characters you have on stage at one time, the more difficult it is to have well-developed characters that interact well with each other.

Before you begin writing dialogue, write a character sketch for each character. Record his or her likes, dislikes, shortcomings and other character traits. List expressions he or she would frequently use. Specify vocabulary and mannerisms that fit the character and make him or her stand out from all the others in the play. The better you define each character before you start writing, the easier the scriptwriting will be.

● ● ●

John did just that. He rented several of Bill Cosby's videos and worked with his puppeteer in developing the voice and mannerisms. He also listed many of the phrases Bill Cosby often says. John was well prepared when he finally sat down to write the dialogue.

Making a Scene

How many scenes will you need? In scripts shorter than three minutes, do everything in one scene. Let the dialogue or additional characters move the plot along instead of using several scenes or time settings to tell the story.

For longer scripts, determine the time frame of each scene, and keep action breaks short—but long enough for necessary backstage preparation. Few scripts should require more than three scenes to complete the action.

In longer skits, plan the two or three scenes so that each character has a resting time and puppeteers have a chance to rest their arms. Also, don't have any one scene last more than five minutes. Otherwise, the puppeteer's arm will tire and the action will slow.

The first scene is vital. The opening needs to grab the audience's attention and get them involved emotionally. Keep action in mind. Have things *happening* on stage, rather than just having characters talk.

As you plan each scene, think about how the scene will look on stage. Write in set changes and props you'll need to make the scene work. But keep your skits practical to perform. Your team may not have access to a potted palm tree to use in a Hawaiian skit, but chances are you can make a cardboard version to create the same effect.

Matching Your Audience

When creating a new skit, make sure the point you're trying to get across is within the mental grasp of your audience. For instance, does the vocabulary you're using fit the age level and background of your audience? It doesn't make sense to talk about political issues with small children or to discuss "life at home" with prison inmates. Also, avoid using

"Christianese"—terminology only longtime churchgoers would understand—unless you're doing it deliberately to make a point.

Have characters speak to the audience on its level. Never have a puppet talk down to an audience or speak over its head. One way to find out how your script comes across is to have individuals preview it and give you their opinions.

The audience's age helps you determine your puppet play's length. This breakdown works well in deciding how long a play should be.

Age	Length
Grades one to three	five to six minutes
Grades four to six	seven to eight minutes
Junior high	10 to 12 minutes
High school and adults	up to 15 minutes

Writing It Down

You know the concept for your play. You know the skit's style and purpose, and who your characters will be. Now all that remains is putting the finished work together and giving it a name.

The planning you've already done has probably taken several days. Use the "Script Planner" on page 59 to help you keep track of your ideas.

Your writing will reflect the quality of your preparation. By first considering the points already covered in this chapter, you should be able to write a complete, unified script in one sitting. Consider these pointers as you begin writing the dialogue.

● Include humor, but don't go overboard. Humor should highlight the message, not obstruct it.

● Repeat important ideas for emphasis.

● Use props and scenery to set the right mood.

● Keep puppets' lines short, emphasizing dialogue and minimizing long speeches.

● Create conflict or tension. Since most lessons in life are born out of conflict, include conflict in your script. Then draw your lesson from it. For example, two guys wanting to date

Script Planner

Title: _____

Intended audience: _____

Purpose: _____

Scriptures that confirm the skit's main idea:

Name of character   Description of character
1._____—_____

2._____—_____

3._____—_____

4._____—_____

5._____—_____

6._____—_____

Expressions or verbal mannerisms each character might use in conversation:

1.   4.

2.   5.

3.   6.

Style or format of skit:

Outline of each scene's action:

the same girl can create a conflict that leads to a lesson on brotherly love or servanthood.

● Stop when you've said enough. Don't prolong a script just to fill time or repeat a point after it has already been made clearly.

● Use adults to handle serious discussion following a play. Puppets are cartoonlike characters. Don't have them act overly serious or perform serious functions such as leading an altar call or praying with kids who want to become Christians.

● Don't depend only on dialogue to carry the message. Include actions that help carry the story.

● ● ●

John's final program contained five short skits that each parodied a popular TV show. Each of the skits had a message about peer pressure or making wise choices in life. And the Dill Crosby character helped tie ideas together between skits and at the program's end. The kids in the juvenile home responded enthusiastically to John's puppet team. A few even approached team members afterward and thanked them for caring.

● ● ●

Practice writing a few simple scripts, and have friends and your puppeteers critique them. Then use their comments as you write more complicated story lines. With practice, you'll soon be writing successful scripts for your puppet team to perform.

CHAPTER 8

All the World's a Stage

"**L**ights! Camera! Action!"

Martin has a habit of calling out that phrase during performances to cue his puppet team to begin a skit or song. That wouldn't be so odd, except his puppet team often performs in parks with no lights and no camera. In fact, the team often uses nothing more than a blanket for a stage. But Martin calls out anyway, "Lights! Camera! Action!"

Once each year, though, Martin's puppet team performs a full-length musical for the community, complete with lighting, sound and, yes, even a video camera. And finally Martin's call makes sense.

● ● ●

Puppet ministry can happen wherever people gather—whether that means an auditorium or a parking lot. Having a nice stage—complete with lighting and sound—can make a puppet team's performance really shine. But doing a skit from behind a dumpster for a group of neighborhood kids can have the same lasting effects on people's lives.

So just what does having a nice stage set accomplish? Sets enhance your program's message. Nothing more, nothing less. Your puppet team isn't crippled if you don't have a nice set. And neither has your team "arrived" just because you do have one.

So design your sets to enhance the puppet team's message, but don't depend on your set to carry the message alone.

Stage Matters

A puppet stage gives puppeteers something to hide behind and spotlights the puppets themselves. With that broad purpose, a puppet stage can be anything from a simple sheet to a multilevel, multicurtain stage designed for grand puppet productions. Choose your team's stage (or stages) based on the number of puppets you use and your audience's needs.

Let's look at possible stage ideas you can use as your puppet team performs and grows.

The refrigerator box stage—In certain cases, you can use a refrigerator or freezer box as a stage. Just lay the box on its side and cut a slit along the top for the puppets to appear through. Because of space limitations, use this type of stage with only one or two puppeteers.

If needed, you can break down the box and carry it to different locations. This type of stage might be ideal for backyard Bible clubs or in situations where a few puppeteers are traveling short distances and doing multiple performances. Since it's made of cardboard, however, this type of stage won't last for more than a few performances.

The microphone stand stage—To create this stage, connect each end of a 6-foot 1×4-inch board to an adjustable microphone stand. You can do this by attaching two metal flanges and two 6-inch lengths of plastic or metal pipe to the board's flat side. This allows the board to sit on the tops of the stands, held in place by the pipes. Use Velcro to hang a curtain along the length of the board. See page 63.

Because you can adjust the stage height easily, this stage type works well for puppet teams with younger kids who're growing quickly.

The improvised stage—Occasionally you may find yourself in a situation where you don't have a real stage to

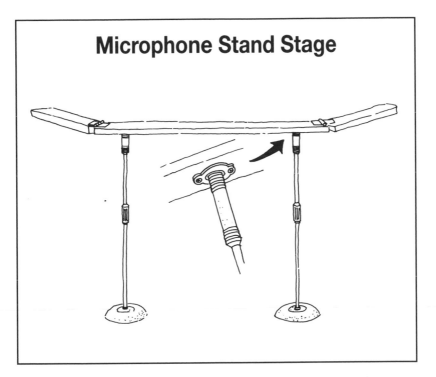

Microphone Stand Stage

work with. If that happens, just use whatever's available. Items such as a pulpit, a piano, a room divider, a chalkboard, a table turned on its side or a blanket held up between two people can all be used as stages in a pinch.

The connected panel stage—This stage is made from three to five panels joined together with hinges. For the panels, use plywood or a wooden framework covered with canvas or fabric. This stage sets up easily but requires a large vehicle for travel. For best results, design the stage so it'll fold flat for travel and storage.

The plastic pipe stage—The most common stage used by puppet ministries today is the plastic pipe stage. This stage uses 1¹/₂-inch diameter PVC plastic plumbing pipe, which is available at lumberyards or plumbing supply stores. The pipe generally comes in set lengths, but you can easily cut them with a hacksaw.

The pipes can be connected to create a two-level performance stage with a backdrop. See the "Two-Level Stage With Backdrop" schematic on page 65. This stage schematic

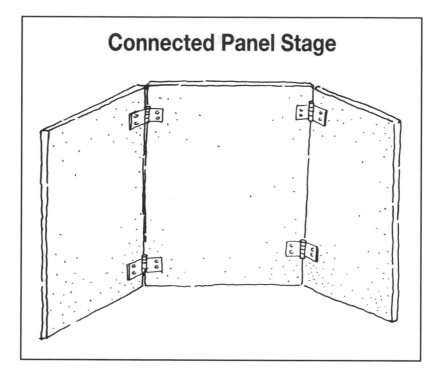

Connected Panel Stage

can also be easily adapted to a single-level stage.

Set the top of the front level at about 48 to 52 inches off the floor, which allows puppeteers to perform in a kneeling position. Set the top of the second level at about 5 feet 8 inches to 6 feet off the floor. This allows a second group of puppeteers to work from a standing position. Also allow two feet of stage width for each puppeteer. For example, if you plan to have three puppeteers on stage at one time, you'll need a stage at least 6 feet wide. Once you know your puppet team's performance needs, you can easily design your own puppet stage using PVC pipe and connectors.

Use a velour, crushed velvet or heavy polyester fabric to form a curtain. Simply sew a casing at one edge of the material so you can insert the pipe through the material. Then slip the curtains over the pipes and assemble the pipes to form the stage (see the illustration on page 66).

Two-Level Stage With Backdrop

Many puppet teams find this stage is the most versatile and least cumbersome to travel with. When fully assembled, the stage can hold up to 10 puppeteers. It also works well for smaller productions that involve frequent scene changes. While puppeteers perform one scene on the lower stage, another group of puppeteers can be preparing for the next scene on the upper stage.

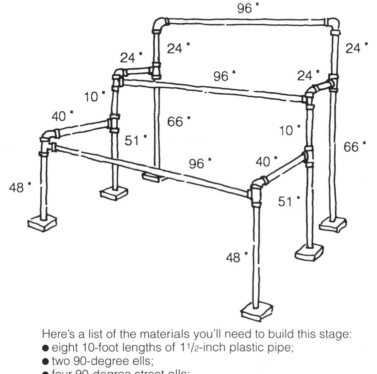

Here's a list of the materials you'll need to build this stage:
- eight 10-foot lengths of 1½-inch plastic pipe;
- two 90-degree ells;
- four 90-degree street ells;
- eight tees;
- six 1½-inch male adapters;
- six 1½-inch cast-iron floor flanges; and
- six wood bases, each 10×10×1 inches.

You may have to adjust the pipes' lengths slightly to make the stage appear level. That's because the pipe connecters vary slightly in length and shape, and can cause the joints to fit differently.

Adapted from *Puppetry Stages*, Copyright © 1983 by Dale VonSeggen. Used by permission.

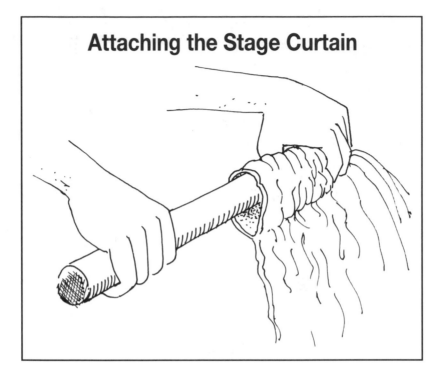

Attaching the Stage Curtain

Once the curtain is in place, use Velcro spots and strips to hold the curtain panels together so no gaps or poorly fitted joints exist.

To hold the plastic pipe framework together, either use duct tape to connect the joints or drill holes through the joints and use nails or bolts to secure them together.

Sound Advice

When you begin a puppet ministry, your team's attention and energies usually go into acquiring attractive puppets and mastering basic manipulation techniques. Your only sound equipment may be a simple cassette tape player.

In the early stages of a puppet ministry, a large "boom box" tape player works well for small audiences. When shopping for a boom box, look for these features:

● a numerical display tape counter;
● input and output jacks;

● bass and treble controls; and

● a pause button.

As your team grows, you'll probably want to invest in a more powerful sound system to enhance your puppeteers' performance.

After all, if the audience can't hear what you're saying, the message isn't getting across.

Sound systems come in all sizes, but for puppet teams the best type is a one-piece, portable system. Several manufacturers make lightweight, compact—but powerful—sound systems with speakers, amplifier and mixer all in one case about the size of a small suitcase.

This type of system works well for puppet teams because it's portable and easy to set up. Most models allow you to plug one or more microphones directly into them, and also connect a line directly from your cassette player.

These portable sound systems can be found at most electronic shops that carry sound equipment. Or try a theatrical supply store.

Beautiful Scenery

Scenery helps set the mood for your presentation. In puppetry, scenery can be draped over the stage curtain or the backdrop curtain, or made to stand alone next to the stage.

You can make scenery out of just about anything. If you'll need a piece of scenery only once, simple cardboard or construction paper may suffice. If you want more permanent scenery, here are four resources you can use.

Foam-cor—Foam-cor is the trade name for a very light but rigid product of the Monsanto Corporation. Its white sheets are made from two thin cardboard pieces with a foam core between. It cuts easily and works well for free-standing props, scenery panels or backdrops. You can purchase it in sheets as large as 4×10 feet.

Polyfoam sheets—Polyurethane foam sheets can be rolled up like carpet, which makes this scenery product excellent for groups that travel long distances. The sheets come in various thicknesses, but generally the $3/8$-inch thick foam works best. You can paint right on the foam with spray paint or acrylic paint. You can also use magic markers to highlight or outline.

The foam sheets attach easily to stage curtains with Velcro. Glue a wide strip of belting material across the top of the foam panel, then sew the Velcro patches to the strip. That way you avoid tearing the foam.

Transparencies—The easiest type of scenery to travel with is projected scenery. Projected scenery requires a rear projection screen set up behind the puppet action and a slide projector or overhead projector to project the scenes. Although ready-made rear projection screens can be expensive, you can make your own using a wood or plastic pipe frame and a screen made from white sheets or a white plastic shower curtain stretched tight across the frame.

Cotton "duck" material—This material works well when you want to paint your scenery right onto the stage curtain. Tempera and acrylic paints both work, and a magic marker can be used to add final touches. Before you paint, however, attach the material to a plywood sheet and lay it flat so the material won't wrinkle and the paint won't run.

Brilliant Lighting

You may be asked to perform in areas that are so poorly lit your puppets become shadows on the stage. Or you may find a script you like that requires special lighting, such as a night scene or a storm. When that happens, you may want to consider purchasing or building a light system.

Theatrical supply houses that sell professional stage lighting equipment usually carry floodlights, spotlights and other equipment, but the cost goes beyond most puppet teams' budgets. Also, this type of professional lighting is designed more for permanent installation and is difficult to travel with because it demands excessive setup and takedown time.

Luckily, most electronics supply stores now carry a wireless lighting control system you can use to build a compact, easy-to-use lighting system.

The system consists of individual modules that the lights are plugged into, and a hand-held control unit. The modules and the control unit plug into electrical outlets, and the signal impulses from the control unit travel through the existing electrical circuitry of the room to control your spotlights.

Always seek assistance from an electrician when building your lighting system. That way you can avoid injuries, accidents and even electrical noise.

Whatever lighting system you use, arrange the lights carefully around the stage area. Place the lights high on the stage's periphery so all shadows cast by the puppets fall inside the stage, unseen by the audience. Also, place the lighting poles to the sides so they don't obstruct the audience's view.

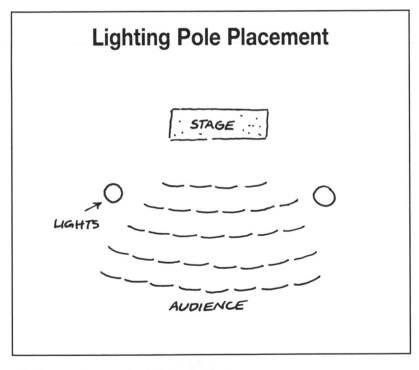

Other Special Lighting

You can use lighting to achieve a variety of special effects. Turn on to these special light sources.

Black light—Black lights require total darkness, a fluorescent black light fixture and fluorescent material or objects. Many puppet groups use black light when doing sign language with puppeteers wearing fluorescent white gloves.

Strobe lights—Strobe lights flash brilliantly at regular intervals. They can be used to depict lightning, stop-action effects or disco-style lighting.

Spotlights—Spotlights can be rented or purchased from a theatrical supply house. Or you can make your own. One inexpensive way to achieve a spotlight effect is to cut a hole in a slide-size piece of cardboard and insert it in a slide projector. Create several cardboard slides with different-size holes and various patterns.

Mirror balls—Create your own mirror ball by cementing small mirror tiles to a plastic-foam ball. When a spotlight or other concentrated light source hits the ball, you get a "starry night" effect throughout the room.

One Step at a Time

Some veteran puppet teams collect impressive arrays of equipment, such as individual headset microphones, walkie-talkies, lighting standards, individually controlled spotlights and black lights, rear projection screens and large, impressive sets with changeable scenery.

Operations of this size obviously entail a great deal of planning and expense, and at times these ministries might "blow away" or discourage a beginning puppet team.

Be assured that special equipment isn't necessary to have an effective ministry. Do the best possible job of ministry with the tools and resources you have. Never purchase "advanced" equipment simply to impress an audience or to be better than another team. If you do purchase advanced technical equipment—such as a lighting or sound system—make sure your motivation is to clarify the message you're presenting and to highlight your puppeteers' skills.

Anyone can put together a slick production. But what matters is that the heart of your message gets across to your audience.

CHAPTER 9

Taking Puppets on the Road

Kermit the Frog sat lazily on his lily pad, strumming his banjo and dreaming about making it in the "big time" world of Hollywood. But the more Kermit played, the more he longed to leave his lily pad and brave the long trip to Hollywood. He wanted to test his mettle in the world of show business.

So he did.

Kermit took off for Hollywood to become a star. Along the way he met a strange mix of friends who joined him on his road to stardom. And when he and his crew arrived, they hit the stage and found success!

● ● ●

That story from *The Muppet Movie* may not be real, but it parallels the stories of many puppet teams across the country who've taken their "act" on the road and found success.

So what about you? After you've performed several times in your area, why not consider planning a puppet ministry tour? Many puppet ministries find that puppet tours help maintain puppeteers' excitement and commitment from year to year. They also help build puppetry skills through concentrated periods of training. Your team's unity and performance skill will increase greatly by focusing the team's energies toward a trip away from your normal surroundings.

Scan these additional reasons a tour can enhance your team's ministry and long-term success:

● Taking your performance to new places gives your team members an added incentive to perfect the details that separate a mediocre performance from an outstanding one.

● A puppet ministry tour provides a great opportunity for spiritual growth. Puppeteers learn to minister to others through their performances and through daily encounters with other team members.

● Many young people never have the opportunity to travel, and a puppet tour becomes the highlight of their year.

● Puppet tours provide great publicity in your home church and encourage potential members to become a part of the church and the puppet ministry.

Setting Up a Tour

The most crucial time of any tour is the time *before* you leave. Tours that aren't planned well are like time bombs waiting to explode. Take the time and energy to set up a detailed tour—including travel route, sleeping arrangements and menus for each day—and your tour will have much less chance of problems.

Determining an itinerary—Before you do any planning, decide on a destination. You can do this effectively by asking your kids where their Christian relatives live. Also check your own family line. Good ol' Aunt Louisa, whom you haven't seen in years, just might be more than happy to host your kids at her church.

Also, look for locations that offer attractions for kids, such as amusement parks or museums. See if you know anyone in that area, such as a minister in a sister church or a one-time church member who has now moved away.

Another option for choosing a destination is to find a church that really *needs* a children's ministry—such as a summer Bible school or backyard Bible clubs.

Remember to listen to your kids too. One leader took his

kids on a trip to Opryland in Nashville, only to find that none of the kids were country music fans. The adults in the group had decided it would be fun, and it was—but not for the kids. Ask your kids what they'd like to do while they're on the road. And plan your route accordingly.

Wherever you decide to go, be sure you have a contact person on the other end—someone who'll be responsible for housing, setup and promotion. If you've set up multiple performances in different towns, secure a contact person in each town. You need someone to be your eyes and ears in each city.

After you've decided on a destination, determine the number of travel days you have available and set an agenda for each day—places you'll visit, sights you'll see and where you'll perform or lodge that evening. Keep your average under 250 miles per day, especially if you're traveling several days in a row.

If you're lodging in a city where you're not performing, call a minister in the area and ask about housing possibilities. Many churches have gymnasiums where groups can sleep. Also, churches may volunteer to house you in their homes even if you don't perform in their church. If neither of those options work, ask the minister to recommend a local hotel.

Planning a tour budget—With proper planning, a tour doesn't have to cost much. When you schedule a performance at a church, ask for four things:

1. Supper and breakfast;
2. Lodging in homes;
3. An offering; and
4. A sincere effort to promote good attendance.

If you can schedule a performance most days of the tour, much of your cost will come from lunches and the fuel for your vehicle. Most tour groups set aside one or two days for fun and sightseeing too. Offerings will help cover all these expenses.

Even if you have to buy all three meals, you can still find creative ways to cut costs. For example, go to a grocery store, buy picnic supplies and eat in a park, or ask host families to fix sack lunches for the following day.

When budgeting your trip's cost, estimate high on your expenditures, estimate low on the offerings you'll receive and charge each puppeteer enough so you'll have money left over to keep your team financially afloat.

Communicating the facts—Mail an information packet with the following items to each church you're planning to perform in.

● a cover letter explaining the tour theme;

● a description of the performance;

● promotional fliers and posters, including a picture and description of your team;

● clarification of what you require from the host church (offering, lodging and meals); and

● a step-by-step explanation of what the contact person must do to prepare for your team's arrival.

Send these packets four to eight weeks before the tour dates.

Communicate with your contact people by telephone to clarify the arrangements. Then mail a second information packet that further clarifies what you're requesting the host church to supply. Also send the contact person a list of the people in your group—including their ages and gender—so the contact person can arrange housing for your puppeteers. Also include information regarding arrival and departure times, so the puppeteers' hosts will know when to pick the kids up and when to bring them back to the church the morning after the performance.

Informing the parents—Schedule a parents' and kids' meeting before the tour to clarify what you expect from each team member. Include your policies regarding:

● amount of spending money needed;

● guidelines for behavior in host homes and churches;

● guidelines for travel in the van or car;

● expectations regarding relationships between guys and girls;

● type of clothing kids need;

● amount of luggage allowed; and

● whether you'll allow personal stereos.

Provide parents with logistical information, such as departure and return times, and a list of items kids will need to pack. Also, consult local medical and insurance agencies to know what forms and precautions are needed to protect against any injuries that might occur. Make parents and kids aware of any legal issues that concern them.

Preparing the troops—Schedule one or two final dress rehearsals before you leave—to make sure you have all the "bugs" worked out of your program. In fact, consider scheduling a "trial run" performance close to home to help your puppeteers build their confidence.

Hitting the road—Consider these tips as you prepare to leave:

● Don't wait until the last minute to pack your vehicle or trailer. Pack it ahead of time to make sure everything fits.

● Make sure your scenery and props are cushioned so they won't be damaged in transit.

● Get *exact* directions to each sponsor church on your route.

Working as a Team

Prior to the trip, assign every team member a specific responsibility for setup and takedown. Responsibilities include: stage setup, sound and lights setup, puppet preparation, ushering, cleanup, and packing the van or trailer after a performance.

Allow time for group prayer before your performance to give kids a chance to express their concerns and requests to God. And seek God's working through your performance. Include your church's host and contact person in this time. Also use this time to encourage team members. Tell them you believe in them and in their ability to minister as God works through them. Your support goes a long way in helping kids strive to do their best.

Making Memories

Your puppet tour should be a *fun* time. Between your performances, schedule fun activities together, such as visiting

Creating Spiritual Impact

Plan meaningful spiritual times for kids while on a puppet tour. Try these suggestions:

● Schedule a "quiet time" each day when kids get by themselves and read the Bible, write in a journal or pray. Provide devotional materials for kids to use during this time.

● Have team members take turns leading devotions during the tour. Schedule group devotions when kids are alert—not right before they go to bed.

● Assign each person a "secret pal" or "secret agent." Challenge kids to make small gifts, share encouraging Bible verses or write special notes to their special person during the tour.

● Schedule a final sharing time near the end of the tour and allow kids to share concerns and blessings. Then pray together and have secret pals reveal themselves.

an amusement park or a water park. Or take your team bowling, canoeing, sightseeing or even shopping at a local mall.

Assign one of the kids to be the tour photographer. Have him or her take lots of pictures or slides of the puppet team at work and at play. Have a "picture party" when you get home and invite prospective puppeteers to join you.

Also, start a few tour traditions. For instance, when your team takes the stage down after each performance, use the discarded duct tape to create a tape ball. Add to the ball after each performance. Then at the end of the tour, present the tape ball to the team member who best exhibited a servant attitude.

Many puppet teams sponsor "coming home" celebrations when the team returns home from a puppet tour. The team performs its puppet production for the home congregation. Then puppeteers share testimonies and memories of the trip with church members. Many teams present a slide show of the tour. Finally, the church members and puppeteers celebrate together with games and a refreshment time.

Think up your own tradition ideas and use them to make your puppet ministry tour even more special.

Puppet tours can be great fun and a great way to encourage kids' spiritual growth. Let guidelines in this chapter inspire you to take your puppeteers on an adventure in ministry. You'll be amazed at the ways your kids grow in their faith and relationships. And you'll be thankful for the way your puppet ministry touches lives.

CHAPTER 10

Avoiding the Puppet Cemetery

Many churches start puppet ministries with great enthusiasm and purpose, only to have them die within six months or a year. To prevent your puppet team's premature demise, let's take a trip to "Polyfoam Garden Cemetery" and read the epitaphs on tombstones of failed puppet ministries. Perhaps you can avoid the pitfalls that've ended the ministries of others.

Cemetery Tour

Here lie the remains
Of cheap puppets and stage.
They gave up the ghost
At a very young age.

Whether you purchase ready-made puppets and stages or make your own, invest your money and energy into resources that will last. Don't plan to just "get by," but plan from the beginning for a ministry that will last many years. Look at the big picture, and not just at your first performance.

Here lies a puppet team
With very little sense.
They failed to choose skits and songs
To fit their audience.

Keep your team's repertoire broad. You can't perform the same material for a teenage group that you would for a preschool children's church. Likewise, a performance at a pastor's convention demands a different thrust than a ministry at an inner-city mission. Audiences range greatly in age, interest and background, and the material you choose for a specific audience should match the needs of that audience.

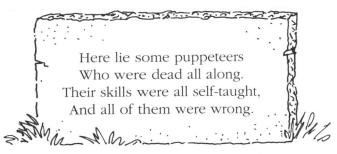

Here lie some puppeteers
Who were dead all along.
Their skills were all self-taught,
And all of them were wrong.

Make sure you learn correct puppetry techniques and skills from the beginning. It's difficult to unlearn bad habits. Puppet ministry has a bad reputation in many churches because of poor techniques and skills. With proper training, excellence will become your team's trademark.

Use these suggestions for learning correct techniques:

● attend puppetry training seminars;

● rent videotapes of proper puppetry techniques;

● visit rehearsals of established puppet teams;

● observe other puppeteers closely on televised puppet shows;

● enter competitions where you'll be evaluated; and

● have team members evaluate each other.

Here lie a bunch of puppets,
And lots of kids too.
They needed just a leader
To tell them what to do.

A puppet ministry leader needs to learn basic puppetry skills to begin training others. Leaders who decide to "wing it" generally find that their puppeteers lose interest because they don't feel what they're doing is excellent or worthwhile.

Here lie puppets galore,
Which show this church's wealth.
It's sad they do no good
Just lying on the shelf.

To maintain interest, a puppet team must remain active and perform regularly. Puppeteers lose interest quickly if all they do is practice. Performing before a live audience provides the positive feedback kids need to develop purpose and excitement.

Here lies a puppet team,
Masters at what they do.
But no one comes to watch them;
They never do anything new.

Many puppet ministries die from sheer boredom. Any puppet skit or song can become boring to the puppet team and to audiences after too much repetition. To maintain excitement and anticipation in rehearsals and performances, continually introduce new material to challenge team members.

Here lie the "might've beens,"
Who never had puppetry chances.
They just sat back and complained
Because they lacked finances.

Although some established puppet teams have many puppets, elaborate stages, sound equipment, lighting equipment, matching shirts and possibly even a van or bus to travel in, these items certainly aren't essential to a group's ministry efforts.

All you need to begin is a puppet or two, a helper or two, something to hide behind and a calling from God to minister. Lack of finances shouldn't be a major problem. Start where you are—with what you have. Do the best you can, and trust God to help you in your areas of need.

Here lies an entertaining puppet team
That loved to tell a joke.
But fun alone without sharing Christ
Has caused this team to croak!

Although puppets can be entertaining, your team needs to present more than just fun and games. In fact, most of the plays, skits and songs you spend time on should be chosen for the biblical message they convey.

Puppetry can be a powerful tool, and what puppets do and say will leave a lasting impression on audiences and puppeteers. Don't waste your group's efforts or opportunities—work together to gain eternal results.

An Ongoing Ministry

The puppet cemetery shows you pitfalls to avoid as your puppet ministry grows. But even avoiding those grave markers won't guarantee success. You need to take positive steps to keep your puppet ministry alive and thriving.

The secret to an ongoing puppet ministry is to motivate team members to take ownership of the ministry and do the best they can with the talents they have. Read these suggestions on how to motivate yourself and your team members to do the best for God.

Earn respect. No puppet team will get far without firm, directive leadership. You must earn your puppet team's respect, both as a puppeteer and as a spiritual leader. Strive to be excellent at what you do. Let kids join with you in directing the ministry, but don't allow puppeteers to control you. Kids need you to be a solid leader so they can explore their own leadership abilities under your guidance.

Use positive reinforcement. Avoid criticism and put-downs. Find something to praise in each team member's performance. Give puppeteers small awards and verbal praise for projects they accomplish successfully. Avoid giving demerits or embarrassing kids in any way.

Perform often. When your team fails to perform regularly, their skills grow dull—along with their motivation to keep working. Scheduled performances give kids goals to work toward.

Keep things classy. A catchy team name and logo, and a flashy business card or brochure will send team spirit soaring. Matching T-shirts for puppeteers are great if you can afford them. Let kids know that what they're doing is important and deserves recognition.

Encourage openness and creativity. Ask your puppeteers for their suggestions for ways to improve as a team. You may not be able to use all their ideas, but giving kids a chance to express their opinions affirms their importance. If your team members seem hesitant to discuss their opinions openly, have them respond to questionnaires you design. Or set up a suggestion box in the rehearsal room.

Encourage long-term commitment. We give a special award plaque to graduating seniors who've served on the puppet team for at least three years. We call it the SWTS Award, which stands for "Staying With The Stuff." Of course, you don't have to use awards, but it's important you recognize kids on your team who've remained faithful to the ministry over several years.

●●●

Puppet ministry provides unique opportunities to minister to hurting people. A puppet isn't threatening. It can open avenues of communication that real people can't. In ways we can't always understand, puppets speak to the child in each of us and help us bring our hurts to the surface for comfort and healing.

Not long ago a puppet team did a program for a group of mentally impaired adults. As the show progressed, the puppeteers were amazed at how the adults opened up to the puppets, treating them almost like new friends.

One adult, Larry, always looked at the ground because he was shy. But when the puppets appeared on stage, he couldn't resist peeking. The puppeteers noticed Larry's curiosity and encouraged him to try a puppet himself. He did.

Eventually, Larry's shy puppet eased onto the stage. Although the puppet never said a word, the puppeteers were deeply moved to see the big smile on Larry's face.

That's puppet ministry. People reaching people through fantasy and fun. Puppets will open doors for ministry that you never thought possible. And with proper guidance and motivation, your puppet ministry will keep growing for many years to come.

CHAPTER 11

Puppet Scripts

Puppets depend on humor to catch the attention of their listeners. However, once they gain the attention of an audience, puppets can be powerful tools to drive home the truth found in God's Word. Use these scripts to reach audiences of all ages with God's love.

Getting in Shape

By Connie Browning

In this skit two friends see the importance of exercising their souls as well as their bodies.

Audience
Would work well for teenagers or adults.

Characters
JANIE—A female puppet or an actress in front of the stage.
STELLA—A female puppet dressed in workout clothes.

Setting
Could take place anywhere.

Stella enters jogging, huffing and puffing. She stops, then begins calisthenics, counting "One, two, three, four." Janie enters, watches Stella, then speaks.

JANIE   My goodness, Stella! What on earth are you doing?

STELLA   (Continues to do calisthenics) Oh, hi Janie. One, two, three, four ... I'm working on the "new me!"

JANIE   (Follows Stella's movements with her head) What's wrong with the "old" you, may I ask?

STELLA   (Continues to exercise) Everything—according to the magazine articles I've been reading.

JANIE   (Still bobbing head) Stella, can you stop for a minute? I'm getting dizzy trying to talk to you!

STELLA   Sure. (Stops and leans back) Whew! What a work out!

JANIE   Okay, now what's all this about a "new" you?

STELLA   You know how everyone is so health-conscious these days. Every time I pick up a magazine, all I read about is the importance of a balanced diet, sufficient rest and exercise. Compared to the models in those magazines, I'm a total wreck.

JANIE   Oh, you aren't in such bad shape. Of course, you need to take good care of your body. But I hope you're planning on spending the same amount of time toning up the inside.

STELLA   (Looks surprised) The inside?

JANIE   Yeah. You're spending all this time and effort getting your body in shape. What about your soul?

STELLA   (Nods assuringly) Oh, my shoes are fine.

JANIE   (Points to her feet, then to her heart) No, not your shoes, your soul—your inner being. Just as your body needs good food to be healthy, your soul also needs nourishment. Unhealthy TV shows, magazines, music—they all add up to spiritual junk food.

STELLA   (A little irritated) Well then, what would good food be?

JANIE   For a healthy soul, you need to meditate on God's Word and spend time with Jesus—the Bread of Life. That's good spiritual food.

STELLA   (Incredulously) Oh, sure. Next you're going to tell me my soul needs exercise too, right?

JANIE   How'd you guess?

STELLA   But how can I exercise my soul?

JANIE   Let me ask you a question. What would happen if you sat on the couch and read books about exercising all day long?

STELLA   (Holds hands straight out) Flab City!

JANIE   But you're reading all about exercising, aren't you?

STELLA   Sure, but it doesn't do me any good just to read about it. I have to get up off the couch and do it.

JANIE   Right! And we exercise our souls when we do what the Word says, rather than just read it.

STELLA   (Thoughtfully) Just knowing what God says isn't enough, is it? We need to be obedient to do all he tells us, huh?

JANIE   (Nods approvingly) Stella, I think you've got it!

STELLA   Janie, I see what you're trying to say. I won't neglect the most important part of me—my soul! Say, how about jogging with me back to the house?

JANIE   (Incredulous) Me?

STELLA   Yes, you! A little exercise wouldn't hurt you a bit.

JANIE   Well ...

STELLA   Oh, c'mon! It's easy! (Stella and Janie start jogging in place) One, two, three, four—that's it! You're doing great! (Jog off together)

Are You Colorblind?

By Dale and Liz VonSeggen

In this skit a puppet discovers how colors can help him understand his conscience.

Audience
Would work well with elementary kids.

Characters
SAL—A live male actor in front of the stage.
JAMES—A young male puppet.

Setting
Could take place anywhere.
You'll need four cardboard circles—one red, one yellow, one green and one blue.

SAL   (In front of stage) Today I'm going to give one of our puppets a test to see whether he's colorblind. (Calls backstage) James, what're you doing?

JAMES   (Enters) Oh, nothing much. What do you want?

SAL   I want to give you a test.

JAMES   (Exits quickly, then says from backstage) Oh, no you don't. I'm not taking any test today.

SAL   It's not a pen-and-paper kind of test. I just want to test your eyes.

JAMES   (Still backstage) Are you sure? (Peeks out)

SAL   Yes. I just want to see if you're colorblind.

JAMES   Well, (Enters) that sounds easy enough.

SAL   (Holds up red circle) If a car driver sees this color traffic light, what should he or she do?

JAMES   Why, stop, of course. Everybody knows a red light means stop.

SAL   (Holds up green circle) You're right. Now, what does this color mean?

JAMES   (Runs across stage and back) It means "Go, man, go."

SAL   Right! What about this one? (Holds up yellow circle)

JAMES   Yellow means . . . "Floor it!"

SAL   Very goo—Uh, now James. You know yellow means "Caution." (Holds up blue circle) Okay, what would this color mean?

JAMES   A blue light? Uh, I don't know. Does it mean "Blue-light special," like at K-mart?

SAL   No, it doesn't. Say, James, did you know that each of us has a set of traffic lights built inside us? It's called our conscience. God put it there.

JAMES   (Points to himself) Traffic lights inside me? I don't get it.

SAL   Well, let's say you have a chance to do something you know is wrong. Your conscience flashes a red light inside you.

JAMES   And you should stop and not do it. But when would your conscience flash a green light?

SAL   Oh, maybe when someone asks you to do something you know you should do, but you don't want to.

JAMES   And the green light means "Go ahead and do it."

SAL   And if you don't, you'd be doing wrong, just like running a red light.

JAMES   You mean you could get a ticket for stopping at a green light?

SAL   Maybe, because you'd be causing problems for those around you. They might run into your rear end. Disobeying gets you into trouble, regardless of what kind of disobedience it is.

JAMES   What would it mean when your conscience flashes a yellow light?

SAL   It means, "Danger, be careful." Suppose you're with friends who're breaking rules or causing trouble. Then the yellow light goes on and tells you to be careful. Be nice, but proceed with caution, and be ready to stop if they get too wild.

JAMES   Okay, I get it. But what about that blue light? I wouldn't know what to do if I saw a blue light.

SAL   Sometimes we get into situations where we really don't know what's right or wrong—just like a driver wouldn't know what to do if he or she saw a blue traffic light.

JAMES   Then what do you do?

SAL   When we get into situations where we can't tell right from wrong, we should ask for God's guidance.

JAMES   And we should ask our parents, youth leaders and friends for help too.

SAL   Yes, they could help. We can also read the Bible and find out what it says about the situation.

JAMES   If my blue light flashes, can I come to you for help?

SAL   Why sure, I'd be glad to help you any time you need some advice.

JAMES   Say, guess what? My stomach is flashing me a green light ... and I know what that means.

SAL   What does it mean?

JAMES   It means "Go home for supper ... I'm empty." (Rubs his stomach) So long. I guess that test wasn't so hard after all.

SAL   Goodbye. And don't run any red lights. (James exits)

JAMES   (As he exits) I'll try not to.

Under Construction

By Carol Simmons

In this skit two new aquaintances discover what Christians are really made of.

Audience
Would work well for upper elementary, teenagers or adults.

Characters
KELLY—An adult standing in front of the stage.
DIRK—A male puppet dressed in construction worker's clothes.

Setting
Construction site.

You'll need assorted construction tools lying in front of the stage. You'll also need two hard hats—one puppet-size and one regular-size—and a sign that reads "Construction area. Hard hats required." Kelly walks in carrying a Bible and discovers the tools, looking puzzled. Dirk enters wearing a hard hat and a flannel shirt.

———————————

DIRK   Hey, buddy. (Waves at adult)

KELLY   Yes? (Turns to Dirk) Were you calling me?

DIRK   Yeah. Where's your hard hat?

KELLY   My what?

DIRK   Your hard hat. (Pounds own hat) Can't you read? (Stops and looks around) Aw, the sign's fallen again. (Looks down) Now where? Yeah, here it is. (Puts sign in place) Now read the sign.

KELLY   (Reading) Construction area. Hard hats required.

DIRK   So where is it?

KELLY	I'm sorry Mr.—? (Asking puppet's name)
DIRK	Tucker. Dirk Tucker.
KELLY	Mr. Tucker, I don't have a hard hat.
DIRK	Oh. Well, hold up a minute. (Drops down and returns with hat. Hands it to Kelly.) You can call me Dirk. I didn't catch your handle.
KELLY	I'm Kelly. (Looks around) Say, what're you building here?
DIRK	Christians.
KELLY	Christians?
DIRK	Yeah. (Shakes head sadly) Ya' know, it seems harder to build Christians these days.
KELLY	Really? Tell me, are you using the right tools?
DIRK	Well, sure. See right here. (Points to tools) Take this hammer. (Picks it up and pounds stage) It's for pounding ideas into Christians' heads. And the crowbar (Picks it up) is for prying them up out of their seats.
KELLY	What about this ruler? (Picks it up)
DIRK	Well, after I build the Christians, I measure 'em with that. If they don't measure up, (Takes ruler and pitches it) out they go. Then there's my hat. That's most important of all.
KELLY	How so?
DIRK	Protection, man. With all the hammering, prying and measuring, pieces of Christians are bound to fly everywhere. This (Pounds hat) keeps me safe.
KELLY	You think so?
DIRK	Why, sure. (Busies himself with tools) Well, I'd better get back to work.
KELLY	You know, Dirk, I think you're using the wrong tools. (Lays Bible on stage) This is the tool you need to build Christians.

DIRK   A Bible? (Laughs lightly) But that's only words. You won't find any hammers in there.

KELLY   But there are words that strike like hammers at people's hearts.

DIRK   Really? (Pauses to think) Well, how about crowbars?

KELLY   There are words in here (Taps Bible) that can pry people out of their seats and into action. (Dirk looks startled) And the whole Bible is a ruler. It's God's measuring stick.

DIRK   I see. Here's where they get thrown out if they don't measure up. Right?

KELLY   No, Dirk. Here's where a Christian asks God's forgiveness and starts to build again.

DIRK   Huh? Start again? (Considers thoughtfully, then remembers hat) But I bet nothin' in there can replace my hat. Yes sir, (Pats hat) protection's the ticket.

KELLY   There's prayer.

DIRK   Prayer, ya say? So, talking to God protects me. (Thoughtfully) Could I borrow your Bible for a while?

KELLY   Sure. (Hands it to puppet) In fact, why don't you keep it? I have others.

DIRK   Yeah? Well, thanks buddy. (Hands hat to adult) Here. I don't think I'll need this now. (Goes off mumbling about tools)

KELLY   So long, buddy. (Removes hard hat, shrugs and exits)

Everybody Ought to Go to Sunday School

By Liz VonSeggen

In this skit our main character discovers the real reason kids should go to Sunday school.

Audience

Would work well for elementary kids.

Characters

V—Ventriloquist. Could also be a live actor in front of a puppet stage.

F—Figure or Vent-pal—referred to as "Zack" in the script. Could also be a moving-mouth puppet behind a puppet stage.

Setting

Could take place anywhere. Best when performed for a children's Sunday school class.

Although this script is designed for a ventriloquist, you can easily modify it to accommodate one live actor and one puppeteer. Just add appropriate stage directions.

———————————

V   Good morning, Zack. I'm so glad you could come to Sunday school with me today.

F   Me too! I love Sunday school! I got lots of friends in Sunday school!

V   What's your favorite Bible story?

F   Humpty Dumpty.

V   Humpty Dumpty? How does it go?

F   There was an egg that fell off a wall and he prayed. But all heaven couldn't put him together again.

V   Are you sure that story's in the Bible?

F Oh yeah! It comes right after Bo Peep.

V No, no. Those are nursery rhymes, not Bible stories. Do you know any Bible verses?

F Sure! Let's see. "If at first you don't succeed, try, try again."

V No, Zack, think again!

F Oh … how about "Two's company, three's a crowd."

V Zack, are you sure you know what the Bible is?

F Wait. Here's my favorite. It's a good one. Listen—"You deserve a break today!"

V Zack, you're really confused. Those aren't from the Bible at all. Two of them are just famous sayings and the last one is a TV commercial for McDonalds.

F (Sings) Go to the golden arches … in your neighborhood. (Stops singing) Pretty good, huh?

V You didn't learn any of those things in Sunday school.

F I sure did! I learned that stuff from my friends.

V Well, Sunday school is a good place to go to be with your friends, but do you ever listen to the teacher when he or she tells a Bible story?

F Like what? Name one. I don't remember.

V Well, the story of Noah, for example. Do you know anything about Noah?

F Oh yeah. Noah and his ark. That's a story about a man and his dog.

V His dog? You don't mean to tell me you think ark was the name of Noah's dog?

F Of course not. Ark is the sound his doggie makes—"Ark, ark ark."

V Be serious, now. Everybody knows an ark is a very large boat. God told Noah to build that boat to save his family and the animals. Now how do you suppose Noah knew how to build that huge ark?

F I bet he studied archaeology!

V No, Zack. That's something entirely different. As a matter of fact, Noah listened to God and did exactly what God told him to do to build the ark.

F Is that why Noah took two of every kind of animal on the ark with him?

V It sure is, Zack. Noah was obeying God. Now then, what does Noah's story teach us we should do?

F I think it teaches us that you got to get married to be safe . . . cause all the singles got left behind.

V No, no, Zack. The story teaches us to listen carefully to God and to obey him. That's how we'll be safe and protected.

F I bet I know something about that story you don't know.

V What's that?

F What was Noah's wife's name?

V Hmmm. I don't know. I don't believe the Bible tells us.

F It was Joan. You've heard of Joan of Arc, haven't you?

V Oh Zack, you really need to read your Bible and pay better attention in Sunday school.

F I remember the story of Jonah and the fish. That's one of my favorites.

V Now we're getting somewhere. You're right. Jonah is a great Bible story. Can you tell me the story the way the Bible teaches it?

F Jonah lived a long time ago. He was a prophet that told people what God told him.

V That's great, Zack! You're exactly right. Go on with the story.

F One day God told Jonah to go to Nineveh, but Jonah didn't like the people who lived there and he didn't want to go to such a wicked city.

V Right again, Zack. So what did Jonah do?

F He got on a boat and went the other way. But on the way he got thrown overboard and a big, big, big fish swallowed him.

V How big was the fish, Zack?

F Well, the Bible doesn't say, but it was bigger than all the fish stories I ever heard.

V Did Jonah die inside the belly of that big fish?

F No. He built a fire to stay warm and waited until the big fish sneezed and then he got out alive.

V Oh, oh. Here you got things a little mixed up, Zack. There wasn't any fire inside the fish, but there was a lot of crying and praying. Jonah told God he was sorry he disobeyed and then God made the great fish spit Jonah out on the shore. And what does this story teach us, Zack?

F It teaches us that people make big fish sick.

V No. No. It teaches us to obey God from the start instead of waiting until we get into big trouble! How do you think Jonah felt in that fish, Zack?

F Down in the mouth!

V You're impossible! Say, Zack, do you have a favorite story from the New Testament? These other two come from the Old Testament.

F I like the parables Jesus told.

V Yes, Jesus was a great storyteller, wasn't he? Which one of the parables is your favorite?

F I like the one where everyone loafs and fishes.

V There you go again. You get the details all mixed up, Zack. That's the *true* story of Jesus taking five loaves of bread and two fish and feeding over 5,000 people. Jesus loved the people and he was living out the golden rule. You see, Zack, we're here to help others!

F Yeah? Then what are the others here for?

V Jesus wants us all to live out the golden rule—treat others like we want to be treated. Your trouble, Zack, is you aren't really listening to your teacher in Sunday school.

F I can't help it. I'm just a dummy, you know.

V Now, now. What's your head for, Zack?

F To keep my ears apart.

V Well, what do you use your ears for?

F Everything the teacher says goes in one ear and out the other.

V Why?

F Cause there ain't nothing there to stop it.

V Well, tell me this, Zack, what do you hope to learn next week in Sunday school?

F The date of the next Sunday school picnic.

V Now listen, Zack. If you don't start listening and learning from your teacher, there's going to be no picnic for you. Will you try?

F You mean stop talking to my friends and try to pay better attention to my teacher?

V You got it!

F I'll do that on one condition. If you can answer a Bible question correctly, then I'll listen better and learn lots.

V It's a deal. What's your question?

F Who was the fastest runner in the Bible?

V Hmmm. I'm not sure the Bible says. I suppose it was Samson because he was pretty strong.

F It was Adam because he was first in the human race. (Laughs)

V That wasn't fair, Zack. That was a trick question. Ask me another one.

F Okay. Who was the straightest man in the Bible?

V This is another trick. Nobody is described as being the straightest.

F Yes sir. Joseph was the straightest man because Pharaoh made a ruler out of him.

V Oh, Zack. This isn't fair. Give me one more chance.

F Fine. Where was baseball first mentioned in the Bible?

V I suppose it was when Cain *hit* his brother.

F No. Rebecca *walked* to the well with the *pitcher*. And the prodigal son made a home run!

V I think it's about time you had a run home. But before we go, could we remind all the boys and girls why we came in the first place?

F Sure! We love Sunday school and we want lots more people to come too!

V But when you come, be sure you listen well enough to get all the facts straight about the Bible.

F (Sings) Everybody ought to go to Sunday school.

V (Sings) Sunday school . . . Sunday school.

F (Sings) The boys and girls and the dummies too!

V No. No. (Sings) The men and the women and the boys and the girls.

F (Sings) Everybody ought to go to Sunday school.

The Light of the World

By Becky Grosenbach

In this skit two characters learn how to let Christ's light shine through them.

Audience
Would work well with elementary kids.

Characters
HUEY—Young male puppet.
FRIEDA—Young female puppet.

Setting
Could take place anywhere.

You'll need one flashlight. Huey enters with flashlight in one hand. He's singing "This Little Light of Mine." Frieda enters as Huey starts second verse—"Hide it under a bushel ..."

HUEY   Hide it under a bushel ... (Shouts at Frieda as she enters) No! (Continues to sing)

FRIEDA   Huey, Huey, take it easy!

HUEY   I'm just standing up for my faith. I'm gonna let my little light shine.

FRIEDA   (In disbelief) Fine. How are you gonna do that?

HUEY   Well, you just push this little switch and the light comes on.

FRIEDA   Cute, Huey, cute. But really ... how are you going to let your light shine?

HUEY   That's the best I can do. I can't hold up my finger like the kids do—for obvious reasons. I have to use a flashlight.

FRIEDA   Do you think that's all there is to letting your light shine? Don't you know what the real meaning is?

HUEY   (Irritated) I have a feeling you're going to tell me.

FRIEDA   Scripture compares the life of the Christian to light. Christians' lives should shine so non-Christians can see the gospel.

HUEY   But doesn't the Bible also say Jesus is the light of the world? Is he the light or are we the light?

FRIEDA   Yes.

HUEY   Yes, what?

FRIEDA   Jesus is the light who lives in us. So we become the light of the world. Our light is supposed to point others to him.

HUEY   So I don't need the flashlight?

FRIEDA   Not unless you're going into the dark. Which brings up another point ...

HUEY   Oh, dear ...

FRIEDA   There are an awful lot of people shining their light where it's not needed.

HUEY   But I thought everyone needed to see the light. How could someone shine their light where it wasn't needed?

FRIEDA   It's kind of like you shining your flashlight here in this room. There's so much light already here, we can hardly see the beam from your flashlight. But if you were to shine it down there ... (Points behind the stage)

HUEY   (Shines light backstage) Oh, yes, it shows up much better down there. It's dark down there.

FRIEDA   Often Christians live like they should at church where the light is already strong. But put them in a situation where they need to take a stand for Christ and their light goes out.

HUEY   So you're saying it's easy to live like a Christian when other Christians are around, but it's harder at school or work when you're by yourself.

FRIEDA Yes, and that's where the light's needed most.

HUEY What about deep, dark Africa? Don't you think we need to take our lights there?

FRIEDA Good point. There are a lot more Christians here than in most other countries. We need to be willing to take our light where it's needed most.

HUEY But if we stay here, we need to keep our light shining all the time. You never know when you'll meet somebody who really needs Jesus' light.

FRIEDA Boy, Huey, I think you've caught on. You seem to really understand this light business.

HUEY Oh, yes. It's quite simple actually. See, you just push this switch forward and then ...

FRIEDA Oh, Huey. (Exits)

HUEY Wait, Frieda. I'll light the way for you. (Exits running after her)

The Interstellar Communication Device

By Pam Towne

In this skit two aliens come to Earth looking for a secret device that allows earthlings to communicate with the Creator.

Audience
Would work well for teenagers or adults.

Characters
TEACHER—An older male or female puppet, or a live actor in front of the stage.
ALIEN 1, ALIEN 2—Two identical puppets wearing aluminum foil, antennae and other "outer space" clothes.

Setting
Church classroom.

TEACHER   Well, it's time to welcome our visitors this morning and ... (Two aliens enter, jabbering to each other)

TEACHER   Well, I know I said visitors, but I wasn't expecting anything like this.

ALIEN 1   (Monotone) Greetings, earthling.

TEACHER   Uh, greetings.

ALIEN 1   We are a special fact-finding delegation from the planet Upahigh. We bring you greetings from our people.

TEACHER   I see. You're from the planet Upahigh.

ALIEN 1   Correct.

TEACHER   And you're here to gather facts about Earth for your planet.

ALIEN 1   Correct, again.

TEACHER   Well, I can understand that. There's a lot to know about our planet. You'll be interested in our government structure, our cultures, architecture ...

ALIEN 2   No, all that is very boring.

TEACHER   Oh, I see.

ALIEN 1   We are interested in the special interstellar communication device you have developed on your planet.

TEACHER   Interstellar communication device? (Embarrassed) Oh, my! I'm afraid you've come to the wrong place. I don't know a thing about communication devices. This is a church. I'll have to put you in touch with NASA.

ALIEN 1   No, no. The signal was tracked to this location.

TEACHER   To this location? There must be some mistake.

ALIEN 2   (Turn to Alien 1) I told you you were wrong.

ALIEN 1   (To Alien 2) Do not nag in front of the earthlings. (To teacher) You have a code word for it. You call it prayer.

TEACHER   Prayer? Oh, well, yes. I guess that could be called interstellar communication.

ALIEN 1   And you use this device at this location?

TEACHER   Oh, my, yes! We definitely use prayer here.

ALIEN 1   (To Alien 2) You see? I was right. Ha-ha-ha-ha.

ALIEN 2   You said not to nag in front of the earthlings.

ALIEN 1   (To teacher) What is this special device called prayer used for?

TEACHER   Prayer? Well, prayer is our way of communicating with our Creator.

ALIEN 1   (Excited) What! You can communicate with the Creator?

TEACHER   Yes, when we pray, we talk to God.

(Two aliens excitedly jabber to each other briefly)

ALIEN 2   This is exciting information. Yours must be a very advanced civilization to have developed such a thing. We must stay and learn these great things from you.

TEACHER   Well, we'd be glad to teach you all we know.

ALIEN 2   Thank you.

ALIEN 1   Everyone on your planet must be very busy communicating with the Creator and learning great things from him.

TEACHER   Well, no. Not exactly.

ALIEN 2   Oh. You have restricted the use of this device to a privileged few.

TEACHER   Oh, no. Anyone may pray who wishes to.

ALIEN 1   So everyone does, of course.

TEACHER   Well, actually, no. To tell you the truth, few people pray. And of those who do, few pray for any length of time.

ALIEN 2   But everyone is allowed to?

TEACHER   Oh, yes.

(Aliens jabber to each other excitedly)

ALIEN 1   I fear that our Earth language translators are not operating correctly. Let me make sure. You have a communication device that allows you to speak to the Creator.

TEACHER   Prayer. That's correct.

ALIEN 1   And the privilege of using this device belongs to everyone.

TEACHER   Yes. Anyone may pray.

ALIEN 1   (Confused) But only a few beings on your planet use this device.

TEACHER   I'm afraid that's true. Relatively few people pray.

(Aliens jabber together for a few moments. Then they begin to exit.)

TEACHER   Hey! Where are you going? I thought you were going to learn great things from us.

ALIEN 1   We made a mistake. Yours cannot be a highly developed civilization.

ALIEN 2   You have a device that allows you to communicate with the Creator, but you do not use it.

ALIEN 1   Yours must be a dull-witted civilization.

ALIEN 2   When you learn to use the great power you have, then we will be back to study and learn from you.

(Two aliens exit jabbering)

TEACHER   (To audience) Hmm. You know, I guess maybe we're not as smart as we think. We have an amazing communication device, but we don't make good use of it. (Exits)

His Hands

By Dale and Liz VonSeggen

In this skit, done solely with hands, the main character discovers that living God's way calls for people to be "real"— not obscured by false identities.

Audience
Would work well for teenagers or adults.

Characters
GREG HANDSOME—White glove with top hat and bow tie.
ROGER RAPPER—Black leather sport glove, such as a racquetball glove.
WAYLON WORKER—Leather work glove.
DOTY DISHES—Rubber glove.
RANDY REAL—Bare hand.

Setting
TV variety show.

Greg Handsome enters by walking on forefinger and middle finger. He waves hand to each side of audience and finally takes a bow to left and right.

GREG   Good evening, ladies and gentlemen. Allow me to introduce myself. I'm the handyman around here known as Greg Handsome. That's right. (Makes an "okay" sign with thumb and first finger) I've got a handful (turn palm up as holding something) of guests to present to you this evening. (Gestures to stage right, where Roger Rapper enters, rapping)

ROGER   I'm bad to the bone; I got the moves. I know where I'm headed; I ain't no fool ...

GREG   (Interrupts) Excuse me. (Roger stops rapping) Could I ask you a few questions?

ROGER   (Starts rapping again) I got no time for your questions; and that's a fact; no time for your questions, so jump back, Jack!

GREG   It's Greg.

ROGER   Huh?

GREG   My name. It's Greg. Not Jack.

ROGER   Oh, sorry, dude. I mean, Greg.

GREG   Could you tell us what you do?

ROGER   Who, me? I'm bad! I entertain ... make people dance ... I do rap ... lots of rap ... I put on a hot show! My audiences move to my groove.

GREG   But sir ... what are you doing of lasting value? Does your show change lives?

ROGER   Sure, man! It changes life! I'm getting super-rich and super-famous!

GREG   Would you consider becoming God's handyman, and working hand in glove with your Maker?

ROGER   Not this rapper! I'm going far! Hey—I gotta go—I gotta $1 million contract to sign. (Exits, making rapping sounds)

GREG   Well, that lifestyle might be glamorous, but I wonder if it's really a meaningful line of work.

(Waylon Worker enters)

WAYLON   Work? Did someone call me? Yup ... if there's any work to be done, I'm the man to call.

GREG   What do you mean? Doesn't anyone else do anything around your church?

WAYLON   Well, not much. I'm the one who really 'complishes things. Why, just last week, I mowed the church lawn, washed the windows, polished the pews and painted the pastor's house. I was at the church 18 different times.

GREG   Wow! Sounds like you've been busy. Real busy!

WAYLON   Sure have. Like I said, if there's anything that needs to be done, I do it.

GREG   Say, have you been spending any time in God's Word? Do you know the Bible?

WAYLON   Oh, no. Been too busy. Lots to do, ya know.

GREG   Well, how about prayer? Do you pray for your pastor? Do you pray about all the work you do?

WAYLON   (Sheepishly) Well ... no. There just aren't enough hours in the day. Say, I gotta go. I'm shampooing the carpet in the reception room today. See ya! (Exits)

GREG   Now there's a guy who's doing good things—but all in his own strength. It makes you wonder what he could accomplish if he had God working with him in all he does.

(Doty Dishes enters, and taps Greg and surprises him)

GREG   Oh, hello! You surprised me! I guess the hand is quicker than the eye. (Laughs)

DOTY   Wah-h-h-h. (Sniffles) Don't make fun of me.

GREG   I'm not making fun of you. What seems to be the problem?

DOTY   Well, everyone puts me down all the time. I try to do something and then everyone makes fun of me. Wah-h-h-h. I tried to sing a song once ... and everyone made fun of me. Wah-h-h-h-h.

GREG   How do you know?

DOTY   (Begins to count on fingers) Well, Sally told Susie and Susie told Mabel and Mabel told Gladys that Alice heard the pastor tell a joke about my singing. So I'll never go back to that church again.

GREG   Well, that doesn't sound very reliable.

DOTY   (Whining) Well, everything I do just flops. Everyone makes fun of me. Nobody appreciates me. I
get no help, I have no money, and I go to that
church at least once a month. You'd think I'd get
better treatment.

GREG   (Sarcastically) Sounds like times are tough.

DOTY   Tough! Do you know what I get to do? Do you?
Do you?

GREG   No, what?

DOTY   Dishes! (Disgusted) I was made to do dishes! Well!
I beat that rap! Ask me how! Go ahead, ask me
how!

GREG   How?

DOTY   I make my husband do the dishes! I deserve to be
treated better.

GREG   You mean you deserve to be handled with kid
gloves?

DOTY   Wah-h-h-h! (Whining) There you go again. All I get
is thumbs down (Turns thumb down) and ridicule.
(Exits as she complains) What I need is just a
handful of TLC—tender, loving care. Everyone always puts me down ...

GREG   Touchy, Touchy! You'd think she'd be a little
tougher than that. Do you suppose we could get
all hands pulling together—entertaining, working,
even stretching to become God's hands in ministry?

(Randy Real enters with force and strength)

RANDY   Yes! (Raise hand) Count me in. (Thumbs up sign)

GREG   (Surprised) Who are you?

RANDY   (Thumb pointing back) Me? (Palm up, fingers forward) I'm the real hand. (Point to sky) God's hand!

GREG   I've never seen God's hand before.

RANDY	(Shaking first finger) Not true! (Make fist) You've seen his hand working—(Shake hands with Greg) making friends, teaching, loving (Put hand around Greg or pat his face) and even preaching! (Reach up high)
GREG	Sure, I've seen lots of hands. What do you think I am—a foot?
RANDY	God needs feet too! (Open palm to sky and then to ground)
GREG	Wait a minute. You're talking to Greg Handsome here. I don't go around begging for handouts, but I could use a few answers! How in the world can you possibly be God's hand?
RANDY	Same as you. (Points to Greg)
GREG	Hold it ... God has all the hands he needs.
RANDY	(Shakes finger) Not true! (Disappears) God has no hands (Appears and points) except yours ... and yours ... and yours. (Lift hand high) Hands up for God!
GREG	I get it! *We* are his hands!

To Tell the Truth

By M. Kurt Jarvis

In this game show skit we discover the difference between real and false Christianity.

Audience

Would work well for elementary kids, teenagers or adults.

Characters

EMCEE—Male, female or animal puppet.
THEO THEOLOGY—Male puppet.
PASTOR PROMPTLY—Male puppet.
MISSIONARY MYRTLE—Female puppet.
CONTESTANTS 1, 2 AND 3—Three female puppets or three live actresses.

Setting

TV game show.
You need the three contestants on one side and the celebrity panel on the other. The Emcee is in the middle. Music, fanfare and applause as Emcee enters.

EMCEE Welcome to our show *To Tell the Truth.* Our celebrity panel for today's show is Theo Theology of Uptown Bible Institute (Theo enters and waves), Pastor Promptly of Downtown First Church (Pastor enters and waves) and Missionary Myrtle, who's on furlough from Outer Southalmania (Myrtle enters and waves). And now we welcome our mystery contestants on *To Tell the Truth.* And as our contestants come out, let's hear from our mystery guest.
(Offstage voice)
Hello! My name is Cynthia Christian. I became a Christian when I was 15 years old. I read God's

Word, pray and try to serve other people and show them God's love in every way I can. (The three female contestants come on stage during voice)

EMCEE   All right, panel, can you guess which contestant is really Cynthia Christian? Is it contestant #1 (#1 waves), contestant #2 (#2 waves) or contestant #3 (#3 waves)? Now, let's question them.

THEO   Contestant #2, can you tell me what makes a person a Christian?

#2   Yes, a Christian is a person who likes other people and does lots of good things. Christians give money to their church and try to live a good life. (Theo scratches his head)

PASTOR   Contestant #1, how do you know that you're a Christian?

#1   I know I'm a Christian because I go to church every week, I teach Sunday school and I go to prayer meeting on Wednesday … and I love my children.

MYRTLE   Contestant #3, there are so many different churches and religions in the world. How do we know which religion is right?

#3   There are many religions and churches in the world, but only one claims that the one, true God became a man so we could know him.

PASTOR   Contestant #2, does being a member of a church mean you're a Christian?

#2   Why certainly. All church members are Christians.

THEO   Contestant #1, does it matter what a Christian believes?

#1   No, as long as the person is sincere, it really doesn't matter what you believe.

MYRTLE   Contestant #3, let's come back to you. Can you tell me who "true Christians" are?

#3   True Christians are those who've accepted Jesus as their Savior and Lord, and have asked forgiveness of their sins. They show their love for God by obeying his Word—the Bible.

EMCEE   Thank you, contestants, for your answers. And now, it's time for our panelists to mark their ballots. (Panelists scribble on imaginary ballots) Now, panelists, tell us who you voted for and why.

THEO   I voted for #3. She knew that God's Word is the basis for all truth.

PASTOR   I voted for #3 too. She knew that the only true Christians are those who accept Jesus as their Savior and ask forgiveness for sin.

EMCEE   Myrtle, how did you vote?

MYRTLE   I voted for #3 also. She knew that going to church and giving money don't forgive sin. She knew that only God forgives sin.

EMCEE   (To the contestants) Well, it looks like we have three votes for contestant #3. (Super dramatic) And now ... will the real Cynthia Christian please stand up. (#2 moves as if to stand up, but sits back down. Same with #1. Finally, #3 stands.)

EMCEE   Well, panel, it looks like you're all correct. It was contestant #3. And that ends our game for today. Thank you, panel and thank you contestants. And now, until next time, remember ... God's Word is the basis for all truth. (Music plays as all exit)

Man-On-the-Go Interview

By M. Kurt Jarvis

In this skit our characters learn how perseverance really does pay off.

Audience
Would work well for teenagers or adults.

Characters
ANNOUNCER—Male or female puppet with headphones.
SPONSOR—Male or female puppet in a suit.
HERKIMER HASSELBAUM—Male puppet with microphone and note pad.
ROCK SUREFOOT—Male puppet with rope draped over shoulder and alpine hat on head.
CHARLIE CHRISTIAN—Older male puppet.
CYNTHIA CHRISTIAN—Older female puppet.

Setting
Skit opens in a radio and TV broadcast station. The first interview takes place on a mountaintop. The second interview takes place in a family living room.

———————————————

ANNOUNCER (Pops up from backstage suddenly) Hello, ladies and gentlemen of our radio and TV audience. You are here again with our man-on-the-go interview brought to you from Station 777 FM, TV channel 7. And now, before we go to our first interview, a word from our sponsor. (Drops backstage quickly)

SPONSOR (Pops up on opposite end of stage) Are you tired? tired? tired? No pep, no energy? Have you got the "poorlies"? Do you feel like someone glued your feet to the floor? Life got you down? depressed? feeling sorry for yourself? Is life one big bummer? Does each day seem worse than the day before? Are you finding aches and pains you never remember having before? Are you looking at life through soot-colored glasses? Does today seem like the last day of the rest of your life? Unhappy? Did your dog look mean at you this morning? Kids got you down? Think you can't go on another minute? If this is how you feel—Boy! are you in bad shape. But, never fear! Hallelujah Pharmaceuticals has the answer for you. The cure-all, the pepper-upper. The pick-me-up! Yes sir! Now available in readable form, that old-fashioned remedy—Scripturemyecin! (Holds up Bible) Proven 100 percent effective in millions and millions of cases. Scripturemyecin comes in book form with verse doses for minor ailments and chapter doses for more serious cases. So! If you are suffering from the misery of misery, don't delay, treat your illness today. Remember, that's S-c-r-i-p-t-u-r-e-m-y-e-c-i-n, Scripturemyecin, available in most homes or your favorite Christian bookstore in the convenient take-along size. (Drops backstage quickly)

ANNOUNCER (Pops up on opposite end of stage) And now—live—our man-on-the-go interview. Today we're featuring Winner's Circle—the success stories. Now, take it away Herkimer Hasselbaum.

(Herkimer enters, microphone and note pad in hand)

HERKIMER For our first Winner's Circle personality, we'll go high on Mt. Heavenrest, where we'll meet Rock Surefoot, this year's gold medalist in mountain climbing. (Enter Rock Surefoot. Someone backstage throws fake snow into the air over the characters. Herkimer and Rock look up in confusion. Then Rock looks at Herkimer.)

ROCK	Hi there, Hercules.
HERKIMER	That's Herkimer.
ROCK	Right.
HERKIMER	Well, Rock! We'd like to talk with you today about your success in the mountain climbing division. Could you tell us how you became successful in mountain climbing?
ROCK	Well, I'll tell you, Horseboomer.
HERKIMER	That's Herkimer.
ROCK	Right. Well, I started as a baby by climbing out of my crib. My mother and father kept putting me back in, but I didn't give up and kept climbing out.
HERKIMER	And where did you go from there?
ROCK	My next experience was in grade school. I attended Heavenrest Elementary—4,600 feet above sea level.
HERKIMER	That must've been an uplifting experience!
ROCK	No, Hazzeldorf. In fact, it was a downer!
HERKIMER	(Under his breath) That's Herkimer! (Normal volume) Ahem! Uh ... oh my. What happened?
ROCK	Well, you see, all the other kids took the cable car bus up to school, but I wanted to be a mountain climber so I climbed the 4,600 feet every day.
HERKIMER	How long did it take you?
ROCK	Seven hours up and 20 minutes down.
HERKIMER	Why such a short time down?
ROCK	I fell a lot.
HERKIMER	Did you get hurt?

ROCK	Sure did! I've had 56 broken bones at last count.
HERKIMER	With so many accidents, how did you ever become a gold medal winner?
ROCK	I never gave up!
HERKIMER	Well, Rock, thank you for your time.
ROCK	Okay, Horkendork.
HERKIMER	That's Herkimer.
ROCK	Right. Be seeing you. (Exits—falls down halfway off set with a crash)
HERKIMER	You okay, Rock?
ROCK	(Offstage) Sure am. Remember, I don't give up.
HERKIMER	(Turns to audience) And now for our last Winner's Circle interview today, we take you to Hometown, U.S.A. and the home of Cynthia and Charlie Christian.

(Enter two puppets)

HERKIMER	Hello there, Cynthia and Charlie!
CHARLIE	Hello, Mr. Hasselbaum.
HERKIMER	Please! Call me Herk! Now, let me ask both of you ... (Looks at note pad) Ah, I see by my information here that you're both the golden crown winners in the Christianity competition.
CYNTHIA	Yes, that's right.
HERKIMER	Could you tell our audience when you first began training for this competition?
CHARLIE	Well, I guess it was about eight years ago. A neighbor of ours introduced us to the Lord Jesus. We asked the Lord to forgive us of our sins and we began to put Christ first in everything in our lives.

HERKIMER	Oh! I see. So you began by becoming Christians and then sort of got involved in the Christian scene?
CYNTHIA	Yes, you could say that.
HERKIMER	Did you find the training difficult?
CHARLIE	(Adamant) Yes, very!
CYNTHIA	(Looks at Charlie) But I think you could say it was enjoyable most of the time.
CHARLIE	Except for that rough period seven years ago.
HERKIMER	Could you tell us what happened?
CHARLIE	Well, you see, after we became Christians, we began giving 10 percent of our income to our local church. That was a little rough at first, but in time we were doing better than ever.
HERKIMER	So what was the problem?
CYNTHIA	Well, about a year after we began tithing, Charlie got very sick, and we ran low on money. But we still felt committed to giving money to God's church.
HERKIMER	That must've been discouraging. What did you do?
CYNTHIA	We didn't give up. We continued to give just as before, and the Lord provided for our needs— and more!
CHARLIE	Then there was the time Cynthia met a young girl who was living on the streets and we took her into our home.
HERKIMER	Oh, boy! That must've been exciting. What happened?
CYNTHIA	She had grown up knowing nothing but distrust and crime. She stole all my jewelry and ran away in the night.

HERKIMER	Now I'll bet that discouraged you.
CHARLIE	Yes, it did. But we didn't give up.
CYNTHIA	I remember one other time when Charlie had to quit his job because his company was doing things we thought were wrong. At the time, I was at home caring for our kids.
HERKIMER	Oh! That's terrible. You mean you had no source of income?
CYNTHIA	That's right. It was about six months before Charlie found another job.
HERKIMER	Now, that must've been discouraging. What did you do?
CYNTHIA	We didn't give up. We trusted God to provide for us through that rough time.
HERKIMER	And did he?
CHARLIE	Oh, yes! People from our church gave us food and money to help us. Just about every week, we had someone inviting us over for dinner. Sometimes we found bags of groceries just sitting on our front porch. Those were exciting days. And all because we trusted God and didn't give up.
HERKIMER	Well, what would you say was the most important factor that got you into the Winner's Circle today?
CYNTHIA, CHARLIE	(In unison) We never gave up!
HERKIMER	And now, after being Christians for several years, if you had some advice for Christians who're having similar problems, what would that advice be?
CYNTHIA, CHARLIE	(In unison) Don't give up! Stay faithful!

CHARLIE	God is bigger than any problem.
HERKIMER	We certainly thank you for your time and advice.
CYNTHIA	You're welcome, Herk!
HERKIMER	(To audience) And that winds up our interviews today from the man-on-the-go. And folks, as you've heard firsthand from our Winner's Circle champions today: If you want to chase away those valley blues; if you're discouraged, lonely, depressed, downhearted, unappreciated, ignored or criticized; and if you have a bad case of the miseries, remember ...
ALL PUPPETS	(Appear on stage suddenly) Don't give up! (All drop out of sight except for Herkimer)
HERKIMER	And now back to our station, TV Channel 7. (Drops out of sight)
ANNOUNCER	(Pops quickly into view) Thank you, Herkimer, for that excellent program today. And now we say goodnight until next time. From all of us here at Channel 7. And from our sponsors, Hallelujah Pharmaceuticals and that cure-all home remedy, Scripturemyecin, keep on prayin' and keep on sayin'—Don't give up! (Drops out of sight)

Puppet Ministry Resources

The following resources represent some of the best available material on puppets and puppet ministry. You'll find many of the books and other resources at your local Christian bookstore. Or you can order them from the publishers.

Books

Handbook of Christian Puppetry by Grace Harp. Aimed at the Sunday school teacher or children's church worker who wants to use puppets in the classroom. It includes some scripts. Published by Accent Books, Box 15337, Denver, CO 80215.

The Puppet Book by Bill Hawes. Includes helpful information on all aspects of a youth puppet ministry. Published by Puppet Productions, Box 9011, DeSoto, TX 75115.

Puppet Director's Notebook by Dale VonSeggen and Jim Scott. Contains helpful advice, record-keeping forms and an excellent merit system for puppeteers. Published by One Way Street, Inc., Box 2398, Littleton, CO 80161.

Ventriloquism in a Nutshell by Clinton Detweiler. Teaches the basics of ventriloquism. It includes exercises and script segments. Published by Maher Ventriloquist Studios, Box 420, Littleton, CO 80160.

Other Materials

Puppet Trax and **Puppets In Concert.** These two cassette tape series contain songs specifically arranged and recorded for puppets. Both series are available from One Way Street, Inc.

Reaching and Teaching With Puppets featuring Dale and Liz VonSeggen. This 90-minute video covers all aspects of training puppeteers and developing a puppet ministry. It includes several performance segments.

Puppetry Suppliers

Baker Book House
1019 Wealthy St.
Grand Rapids, MI 49506

Maher Ventriloquist Studios
Box 420
Littleton, CO 80106

One Way Street, Inc.
Box 2398
Littleton, CO 80161

Puppet Pals
100 Belhaven Dr.
Los Gatos, CA 95030

Puppet Productions
Box 9011
DeSoto, TX 75115

Son Shine Puppet Co.
Box 6203
Rockford, IL 61125

The Train Depot
5015 Tampa West Blvd.
Tampa, FL 33634

Organizations

Fellowship of Christian Magicians
Box 232
Sterling,CO 80751

Fellowship of Christian Puppeteers
Box 483
Bridgeville, PA 15017

North American Association of Ventriloquists
Box 420
Littleton, CO 80160

Puppeteers of America
5 Cricklewood Path
Pasadena, CA 91107

Ventriloquism

Ventriloquism provides a unique way for one person to grab an audience's attention. And contrary to common opinion, ventriloquism isn't an art form limited to a few gifted people.

But just what is a ventriloquist? A ventriloquist is someone who brings the illusion of life to an inanimate object. This involves:

- carrying on a two-way conversation in which the ventriloquist makes it appear he or she has no control over what the "dummy" says;
- creating an appealing character that doesn't act or sound anything like the ventriloquist;
- moving the vent-pal to give the illusion that it could jump down and move on its own power; and
- keeping his or her mouth still while the character is talking.

Choose your partner. When you think of a vent-pal, you probably think of a wooden puppet character. But don't overlook the possibilities of a full-bodied cloth vent-pal. Consider the comparison on page 126 when deciding between the two types.

Watch your mouth. Lip control takes practice, but most people can catch on quickly. Just to get the feel of it, stand in front of a mirror. Close your mouth and place your teeth together, but don't clench them tightly. Next, part your lips slightly. You want your mouth to appear almost closed.

Vent-Pal Comparison

Advantages of a full-bodied cloth puppet
- **Realism**—Moving the head from side to side causes the rest of the body to move naturally with it.
- **Mouth movement**—Manipulating the mouth of a cloth figure is much easier than working the levers and strings of a wooden figure.
- **Weight**—Cloth characters are much lighter than wooden ones.
- **Dependability**—Wooden characters may have mechanical difficulties such as sticking mouths, broken strings or cracked parts. Cloth figures may wear out, but they'll never break while you're performing.
- **Cost**—Cloth figures are considerably less expensive than wooden figures.

Advantages of a wooden puppet
- **Animation**—A wooden puppet can simulate more lifelike characteristics. For example, winking, rolling its eyes, raising its eyebrows, shaking hands, closing its eyes or sticking out its tongue.
- **Durability**—A wooden puppet's face can be repainted—and repairs can be made—to maintain the character for the life of the ventriloquist.
- **Recognition**—Most people think of a wooden puppet as the standard for ventriloquism. Audiences may expect a ventriloquist to perform with the traditional character and may be disappointed if the ventriloquist uses only soft puppets.

In this position, try pronouncing the ventriloquist's easy alphabet without moving your lips. None of the following letters require lip movement. Say each letter distinctly, using tongue action but no lip movement: A, C, D, E, G, H, I, J, K, L, N, O, Q, R, S, T, U, X and Z.

Practice the easy alphabet in your natural voice and then try it with a character voice. Next, try the dialogue on page 127, which uses mostly easy letters for your vent-pal.

Remember to change your voice to fit your partner, and practice until you are comfortable making voice changes and maintaining good lip control.

The remaining letters in the alphabet—B, F, M, P, V, W and Y—require more work to perfect. The secret to these let-

---

Sample Dialogue

"V" represents you, the ventriloquist, and "F" represents the figure. These letters are common for ventriloquism scripts.

V: Good morning, _____. I'm so glad you could visit our youth group today.

F: Yeah, sure . . . (looks at V) Howdy, stranger.

V: Stranger? It's me, _____. I'm your buddy, pal, friend. Remember me—the guy that puts words in your mouth. I'm no *stranger*.

F: You're stranger than anyone else I know!

V: Okay, all right. So I'm a little off the wall from time to time. But right now I need a little help.

F: I'd say you could use lots of it.

V: Well then give me a hand, would ya?

F: Okay . . . (turns to audience) Let's hear it now! Here's the guy who needs a hand!

V: Hold it! You're supposed to be helping me announce our group outing Saturday night.

F: What we need are strangers.

V: Not strangers. Visitors. (turns to audience) We want you to bring your friends to the party next Saturday night.

F: (sings to the tune of "Strangers in the Night") Strangers Saturday night . . .

V: So what time is it?

F: Six o'clock.

V: Where do we meet?

F: At the church.

V: We hope you'll all be there with a stranger . . . I mean a *friend*!

F: See you Saturday!

---

ters lies in sound substitution and lots of practice. Look at "Sound Substitutions" on page 128, and practice the new sounds. As you substitute the letters indicated, *think* the sound of the letter you want to produce.

For additional help, check out *Success With Ventriloquism* by Liz VonSeggen. This audio cassette offers step-by-step directions for how to become a ventriloquist. It's available from One Way Street, Inc., 1-303-790-1188.

Sound Substitutions

Letter	Substitution	Examples
F	Th	fun = <u>th</u>un fantastic = <u>th</u>antastic of = o<u>th</u>
V	Th	very = <u>th</u>ery value = <u>th</u>alue victory = <u>th</u>ictory
Y	U	yes = <u>u</u>es you = <u>u</u>ou yellow = <u>u</u>ellow
W	$\overline{oo}$, as in "boo" plus the vowel sound in the word	water = $\overline{oo}$ + ahter wet = $\overline{oo}$ + et wife = $\overline{oo}$ + ife
M	N + NG, as in the ending of "sing"	money = n + ngoney Mike = <u>N + ng</u>ike hamster = <u>han + ng</u>ster
P	T(h), emphasis on the "T"	paint = <u>t(h)</u>aint park = <u>t(h)</u>ark pear = <u>t(h)</u>ear
B	T(h)	boys = <u>t(h)</u>oys basketball = t<u>(h)</u>asket<u>t(h)</u>all Betty = <u>T(h)</u>etty